P9-DCM-245

Freedom of
SIMPLICITY

Richard J. Foster

HarperSanFrancisco
A Division of HarperCollins*Publishers*

To

Dallas Willard

whose life reflects
the grace of simplicity
in all its manifold complexity

All Scripture quotations, unless otherwise noted, are from the
Revised Standard Version of the Bible, copyrighted © 1946, 1952,
© 1971, 1973.

FREEDOM OF SIMPLICITY. Copyright © 1981 by Richard J. Foster.
All rights reserved. Printed in the United States of America. No
part of this book may be used or reproduced in any manner whatsoever without written permission except in the case of brief
quotations embodied in critical articles and reviews. For information address HarperCollins Publishers, 10 East 53rd Street, New
York, NY 10022.

Designed by Donna Davis

FIRST HARPER & ROW PAPERBACK EDITION PUBLISHED IN 1989.

Library of Congress Cataloging-in-Publication Data

Foster, Richard J.
    Freedom of simplicity.
      1. Simplicity. I. Title
BJ1496.F67 1981   234'.1   80-8351
ISBN 0-06-062832-4
ISBN 0-06-062825-1 (pbk.)

92 93 BANTA 10 9 8 7 6

CONTENTS

PREFACE

This is not a book that I was automatically drawn to write. I was, in fact, brought all but kicking and screaming to this task. I did in the end write it, but it is perhaps not irrelevant to note the reasons for my hesitancy.

First, there was the matter of my own experience in simplicity, or lack thereof. Did I know enough of the inner reality of simplicity to write with any degree of integrity? How deeply rooted was I in this life of unhurried peace and power? And then there was the matter of lifestyle. My family and I still struggle with decisions about money and possessions. By no stretch of the imagination do we have the final answer on what to buy or what to do without. And what about the corporate nature of simplicity? How could I, with any measure of competence, address the tangled issues of economics and world hunger and international trade? I felt, and do feel, like a beginner in all the varied aspects of simplicity.

Second, I hesitated because I know that Christian simplicity is a terribly complex matter. That is understandable, if paradoxical. Seldom in life is there any issue of significance that will yield to easy answers. Not only must we understand the biblical witness to simplicity and the rich tradition of the devotional masters, but we must interact with the contemporary issues. Further, it is necessary to boil all these matters down into the practical world in which we live—a world of schedules and demands, a world of bills and budgets. And this is no simple task.

Third, I was concerned about the danger of legalism. Simplicity is the most outward of all the Disciplines, and hence the most susceptible to corruption. How could I be specific without being rigid? How could I call people from greed without introducing a new pharisaism?

I had a fourth reason that made me cautious about writing a book on simplicity. Of the four, this one was my greatest concern, and the one to which I give attention in Chapter 1.

ACKNOWLEDGMENTS

Anyone who writes knows that an author's family always bears the greatest burden of sacrifice in the publication of a book. My wife, Carolynn, bore patiently my year-long obsession with the topic of simplicity. During the final months of writing, she took over all of my responsibilities at home and literally was mother and father to our boys. I thank her. Joel and Nathan were keenly interested in the progress of the book, and somehow always seemed to understand when the soccer game with Dad had to be cut short. I now look forward to many exciting and lengthy soccer games, even if I continue to lose every one of them.

The relationship between an author and an editor is unique. Roy M. Carlisle, my editor at Harper & Row, has an unusual ability to guide without dominating, to encourage without flattering, and to correct without discouraging. On several occasions his perceptive comments have opened up an entirely new creative direction for the book, for which I am grateful.

I was privileged to attend the International Consultation on Simple Lifestyle held at Hoddesdon, England, in March of 1980. The many Christian friends from around the world whom I met at that gathering helped me to see the infinite variety of faithful witnesses to the life of simplicity.

My deep appreciation goes to Dorothy Craven, Professor of English, Emeritus, at Friends University, who read the entire manuscript and made many helpful suggestions. My thanks also to a small literary group at Friends University who listened as I read much of the text of this book and encouraged me in its writing.

Numerous people read all or part of the manuscript and gave valuable suggestions. They include Kenneth Boulding, Harold Friesen, Verlin Hinshaw, Howard Macy, Raymond Nelson, and Tom Rozof. My thanks to Leroy Brightup and Harold Cope, who encouraged me throughout this project; and to Marilyn Pitts and Wanda Payne, who did the typing.

These and the many others who have surrounded my life have helped give shape to this book. I owe them an immense debt. They are the living voice of the Church—*vita vox ecclesiae.*

PART I

The Foundation

1. THE COMPLEXITY
OF SIMPLICITY

Seek simplicity—and distrust it.
    —Alfred North Whitehead

Contemporary culture is plagued by the passion to possess. The unreasoned boast abounds that the good life is found in accumulation, that "more is better." Indeed, we often accept this notion without question, with the result that the lust for affluence in contemporary society has become psychotic: it has completely lost touch with reality. Furthermore, the pace of the modern world accentuates our sense of being fractured and fragmented. We feel strained, hurried, breathless. The complexity of rushing to achieve and accumulate more and more frequently threatens to overwhelm us; it seems there is no escape from the rat race.

Christian simplicity frees us from this modern mania. It brings sanity to our compulsive extravagance, and peace to our frantic spirit. It liberates us from what William Penn called "cumber." It allows us to see material things for what they are—goods to enhance life, not to oppress life. People once again become more important than possessions. Simplicity enables us to live lives of integrity in the face of the terrible realities of our global village.

Christian simplicity is not just a faddish attempt to respond to the ecological holocaust that threatens to engulf us, nor is it born out of a frustration with technocratic obesity. It is a call given to every Christian. The witness to simplicity is profoundly rooted in the biblical tradition, and most perfectly exemplified in the life of Jesus Christ. In one form or another, all the devotional masters have stressed its essential nature. It is a natural and necessary outflow of the Good News of the Gospel having taken root in our lives.

While it is important to stress that Christian simplicity is more than a mere reaction to the modern crisis, it should also be underscored that simplicity is keenly relevant to the massive problems of our world. We are witnessing poverty and starvation on a scale unprecedented in human history. By the time we fall asleep tonight another ten thousand individuals will have died of starvation—over four hundred per hour. Many more millions live on the brink of extinction—malnourished, aimless, desperate. It is difficult to relate to statistics, even when we know they represent precious ones for whom Christ died. But it is not hard to relate to the story of a man such as Kallello Nugusu, who had to sell his two oxen in order to buy food to keep his wife and six children alive when the famine struck Ethiopia. He then had no way to plow his fields and plant his crops, and the food was gone. When asked what he would do, he responded that he didn't know. Then, dropping his head into his hands, he said, "When my children cry because they are hungry, then it is very hard to be a father."[1]

Though such accounts touch us deeply, we often feel helpless to do anything. How can we respond with any degree of integrity and effectiveness? It is the Discipline of simplicity that gives us the basis for developing a strategy of action that can address this and many other social inequities. Individual, ecclesiastical, and corporate action can spring from the fertile soil of simplicity.

We also struggle with the problem of competing responsibilities that all demand our attention. Like Jack's beanstalk, our obligations seem to grow overnight. We are trapped in a rat race, not just of acquiring money, but also of meeting family and business obligations. We pant through an endless series of appointments and duties. This problem is especially acute for those who sincerely want to do what is right. With frantic fidelity we respond to *all* calls to service, distressingly unable to distinguish the voice of Christ from that of human manipulators. We feel bowed low with the burden of integrity.

But we do not need to be left frustrated and exhausted from the demands of life. The Christian grace of simplicity can usher us into the Center of unhurried peace and power. Like Thomas Kelly, we can come to know by experience that God "never guides us into an intolerable scramble of panting feverishness."[2] In simplicity, we enter the deep silences of the heart for which we were created. Pope John XXIII declared, "The older I grow the more clearly I perceive the dignity and winning beauty of simplicity in thought, conduct, and speech: a desire to simplify all that is complicated and to treat everything with the greatest naturalness and clarity."[3]

Complex Simplicity

While simplicity provides an answer to the modern dilemma, it does not provide an *easy* answer. We must never confuse simplicity with simplism. If you came to this book in the hope of finding four easy steps to total simplicity, you will be sadly disappointed. Simplistic answers, by their very nature, fail to perceive the rich, ordered complexity of life.

Whether we peer into the universe of the telescope or the universe of the microscope, we cannot help being amazed at the varied complexity of the created order. From galaxy to ant to atom we are awed by the intricate mosaic. The apparatus inside our head is literally inconceivable in its complexity, containing perhaps a hundred billion neurons. And beyond that is the mystery of human consciousness, which baffles the imagination. As the Psalmist declared, we are indeed "fearfully and wonderfully made."

Christian simplicity lives in harmony with the ordered complexity of life. It repudiates easy, dogmatic answers to tough, intricate problems. In fact, it is this grace that frees us sufficiently to appreciate and respond to the complex issues of contemporary society. The duplicitous mind, on the other hand, tends to confuse and obscure. While the dogmatic person cannot understand the diversity in simplicity, the double-minded person cannot perceive the unity in complexity.

This brings us to the central paradox of our study: the complexity of simplicity. The fact that a paradox lies at the heart of the Christian teaching on simplicity should not surpise us. The life and teachings of Christ were often couched in paradox: the way to find our life is to lose it (Matt. 10:39); in giving we receive (Luke 6:38); he who is the Prince of Peace brings the sword of division (Matt. 10:34). Those with simplicity of heart understand the Lord, because much of their experience resonates with paradox. It is the arrogant and the obscurant who stumble over such realities.

Paradoxes, of course, are only apparent contradictions, not real ones. Their truth is often discovered by maintaining a tension between two opposite lines of teaching. Although both teachings may contain elements of truth, the instant we emphasize one to the exclusion of the other the truth becomes distorted and disfigured. We can see this easily enough when we insist—rightly I think—that God is both imminent and transcendent, both in the created order and beyond the created order. If we stress imminence to the exclusion of transcendence, we end up with some form of pantheism. Conversely, if we stress transcendence to the exclusion of imminence, we will end up with a detached, disinterested, wind-the-clock-up kind of God. If we embrace either end of the teaching exclusively, we get a distortion; if we hold both in tension, we find the God of Abraham, Isaac, and Jacob. We could just as easily take concepts such as the love and justice of God, the deity and humanity of Christ, or any one of the number of examples that abound in the Scripture.* Let us consider some of the complex aspects of simplicity that we must keep in proper tension if we are to enter into this important Christian virtue.

A pivotal paradox for us to understand is that simplicity is both a grace and a discipline. An old Shaker hymn articulates this double reality with amazing clarity. Joyfully, there is the affirmation,

> 'Tis a gift to be simple,
> 'Tis a gift to be free.

---

* Though not central to the present discussion, it should nevertheless be noted that some paradoxes involve keeping more than two lines of teaching in tension. The doctrine of the Trinity, for example, involves three separate teachings which must be kept in undivided tension if we are to do justice to the biblical record. Incidentally, it is only in this perfect tension that we see the profound unity in the Godhead. It is the example *par excellence* of complex simplicity.

as well as the assertion that we must,

> Turn and turn,
> Till we turn 'round right.

Simplicity is a grace because it is given to us by God. There is no way that we can build up our willpower, put ourselves into this contortion or that, and attain it. It is a gift to be graciously received. By way of illustration, the story is sometimes told of Hans the tailor. He had quite a good reputation, and so when an influential entrepreneur in the city needed a new suit he went to Hans requesting one be tailor-made. But the next week when he came to pick it up, the customer found that one sleeve twisted this way and the other that way, one shoulder bulged out and the other caved in. He pulled and struggled until finally, wrenched and contorted, he managed to make his body fit the strange configuration of the suit. Not wanting to cause a scene he thanked the tailor, paid his money, and caught the bus for home. A passenger on the bus, after surveying the businessman's odd appearance for some time, finally asked if Hans the tailor had made the suit. Receiving an affirmative reply, he remarked, "Amazing! I knew that Hans was a good tailor but I had no idea he could make a suit to fit perfectly someone as deformed as you." Just like the entrepreneur, we often get an idea of what simplicity should look like and then we proceed to push and shove until, bruised and battered, we "fit." But that is not the way simplicity comes. It slips in unawares. A new sense of wonder, concentration, even profundity steals into our personality. We change our lifestyle, even taking up the ministry of poverty when it is clearly right and good, out of inner promptings, knowing that when the call is made the power is given. The tailor-made fit is perfect. Simplicity is a grace.

Of course, we must not forget the other pole of our tension, for simplicity is also a discipline. It is a discipline because we are called to do something. Simplicity involves a consciously chosen course of action involving both group and individual life. What we *do* does not give us simplicity, but it does put us in the place where we can receive it. It sets our lives before God in such a way that he can work into us the grace of simplicity.

It is a vital preparation, a cultivating of the soil, a "sowing to the Spirit," as Paul put it.

Perhaps we need to learn to speak of "disciplined grace." Isn't that the profound reality which underlies the symbiotic alliance between faith and works? Our salvation is *sola fide*, by faith alone, but without works faith is dead. The Gospel reality comes to us by pure grace, but it bears the mark of spiritual discipline.

A second, closely aligned paradox regarding Christian simplicity is that it is both easy and difficult. It is easy in the same way in which all Christian graces, having once worked their way into the ingrained habit structure of our lives, are easy. It is easy in the way that breathing is easy. "Virtue is easy," say the moral philosophers, and so it is once it is embedded in the personality. The playing of Tchaikovsky's *Pathétique* is easy to the accomplished musician who has labored until it flows out in his very body language; but until then it is difficult, painfully difficult. And in simplicity there are times of struggle and effort, times when we despair of ever having our lifestyles where we feel they should be, times when we wonder if our lives will ever be of one piece. But occasionally, in the middle of the struggle, we have a sense of entering in, and spontaneously we glorify our Father in heaven because we know that we have done no more than to receive a gift.

A third tension we must work to keep in balance is between the inner and outer dimensions of simplicity. Simplicity is an inward reality that can be seen in an outward lifestyle. We must have both; to neglect either end of this tension is disastrous.

If simplicity were merely a matter of externals, things would be quite easy. We would then need only to formulate the system (no small trick to be sure) that defines the boundaries— Christian faithfulness would allow us to live in this income bracket but not that one, to purchase this house but not that one. We would have a clearly definable arrangement, even if it would need periodic adjustment to keep abreast of inflation. It would be clear who is in and who is out, who is faithful and who is not. Presto, a new pharisaism. Very fine, thank you.

Sometimes I genuinely wish it were that way. And I have no

desire to speak disparagingly of the many groups who have developed such systems. In fact, I envy them at times, because the clarity of that approach has immense power to motivate and change behavior. But as we all know, its end result is bondage and death. The letter always kills; the Spirit alone gives life. Gospel simplicity gives freedom and liberation.

The outer expression of simplicity must flow from the inner resources. It is learning to walk in the Spirit that builds the life of purity, unity, and grace. There is an inwardness that is central to our task; without it all is lost. We delude ourselves, however, if we think we can possess the inner reality of simplicity without its having a profound effect upon the way we live; the tension must be maintained.

Perhaps you have noted that I have been dealing with the age-old continuum of legalism to license. We reject legalism because it leads to spiritual suicide, and we reject license for the same reason. There is another way—the life of the Spirit. The Apostle Paul gives the classic formulation of this reality in his Epistle to the Galatians. There he came down about as hard as he possibly could against casuistic legalism and for the glorious freedom that we know in Christ, perceptively adding that we must not allow our freedom to be an opportunity of the flesh. He concludes, "If we live by the Spirit, let us also walk by the Spirit" (Gal. 5:25). If we possess the inward reality, it must manifest itself in an outward lifestyle.

A fourth paradox in simplicity is seen in the affirmation of both the goodness and the limitation of material things. The material world is good, but it is a limited good—limited in the sense that we cannot make a life out of it. To deny the goodness of the created order is to be an ascetic. To deny the limitation of the created order is to be a materialist.

The Christian faith views material things as created goods God has given us to enjoy. It does not dismiss material things as inconsequential, or worse yet, as evil. The material world is good and meant to make life happy. In fact, adequate provision is an essential ingredient in the good life. In human society today, misery often arises from a simple lack of provision.

Misery also arises when people try to make a life out of provision. While it is an essential ingredient in the good life, it is by no means the only ingredient, nor is it even the most important one. So often the biblical teaching on provision has been taken and twisted into a doctrine of gluttonous prosperity. All the subtle, and sometimes not so subtle, coaxing to "love Jesus and get rich" reflects our failure to see the biblical limitation upon things. Incarnated into our theology are covetous goals under the guise of the promises of God. And the interesting thing about all these little gimmicks to blessedness is that they work, they really do work. That is, they work if what we want is a little money; but if we desire the abundance which God gives, they fail.

Again, we see that Christian simplicity does not yield to simplistic answers. The tension must be maintained: things are good, but that good is limited.

Perhaps one more example of paradoxical tension will be sufficient to emphasize the fact that our journey into simplicity will be as intricate, varied, and rich as human personality itself. I refer to the attractive ability to be single-hearted and at the same time sensitive to the tough, complex issues of life. It is a strange combination and quite difficult to explain, though quite easy to recognize. There is focus without dogmatism, obedience without over-simplification, profundity without self-consciousness. It means being cognizant of many issues while having only one issue at the center—holy obedience.

Jesus spoke to the heart of the matter when he taught us that if the eye were single, the whole body would be full of light (Matt. 6:22). Dietrich Bonhoeffer, before he died at the hands of the Nazis, said, "To be simple is to fix one's eye solely on the simple truth of God at a time when all concepts are being confused, distorted, and turned upside down."[4] Such focus makes one decisive and able to cut through the Gordian knots of life.

But we must never confuse the clear decisiveness of the single-hearted with the simplistic decisiveness of the propagandist. While propagandists have a singleness of purpose that is often quite amazing (and baffling), they do not enter it by the same path as the single-hearted. In joyful abandon they pontificate on politics, religion, and philosophy, without the slightest awareness or concern for the intricacies involved. At times they may come to exactly the same conclusion as the single-hearted, and may even express it in the same words and with the same conviction. But they came to the conclusion too quickly, too easily. It is hollow because it lacks the integrity of painful struggle.

Have you ever experienced this situation? One person speaks, and even though what he or she is saying may well be true you draw back, sensing the lack of authenticity. Then someone else shares, perhaps even the same truth in the same words, but now you sense an inward resonance, the presence of integrity. What is the difference? One is providing simplistic answers, the other is living in simplicity.

The Part and the Whole

Oversimplification is a danger in any field of study. But the danger is especially insidious in the study of Christian simplicity, because it can so easily be viewed as a virtue. We have touched on a few pitfalls; however, we have not yet mentioned the area of greatest peril: the danger of assuming that simplicity can function independently of the rest of Christian devotion. Simplicity is the most outward of all the Spiritual Disciplines and therefore the most susceptible to corruption, and the greatest corruption is to isolate it. It was this danger that prevented me for many months from consenting to write a full-length book on the subject. I had written about simplicity before, but always in the context of the Classical Disciplines of the Spiritual Life.[5] There it was integrated into the whole of Christian devotion; it was only a part, howbeit a vital part, of something much larger, more comprehensive.

Simplicity needs to be seen in the light of the whole. For example, there is an intrinsic relationship between simplicity and prayer, especially that central aspect of prayer which is trust. My children love pancakes, so once in a while I get up early to fix them a batch. It is interesting to watch those boys. They wolf down pancakes as if there were an endless supply. They are not worried one whit about the price of eggs or my ability to provide them with pancakes. Not once have I seen them slipping some into their pocket thinking, "I don't know about Dad; I had better put away a little stash so that I can be sure of pancakes tomorrow." As far as they are concerned, the reservoir of pancakes is infinite. All they need to do is ask and, if it is in their best interest, they know they will receive. They live in trust. And without this spirit of trust we will find it exceedingly difficult (should I say impossible?) to live on the basis of prayer for daily bread. No, we will need an adequate stash somewhere, just in case—and be assured that what we now have is *never* adequate.

Paul counseled Christians to live free from anxiety. That, of course, is more easily said than done. Everything in our training and in our culture combats a carefree spirit of unconcern. How can we be free from anxiety? What resource is available to us? Paul perceived the resource to be prayer: "Have no anxiety about anything, but in everything by prayer and supplication with thanksgiving let your requests be made known to God" (Phil. 4:6). Prayer frees us from anxiety because it teaches us trust. And the result is peace: "And the peace of God, which passes all understanding will keep your hearts and minds in Christ Jesus" (Phil. 4:7). Prayer and simplicity are intertwined.

Again, simplicity and solitude walk hand in hand. Solitude refers principally to the inward unity that frees us from the panicked need for acclaim and approval. Through it we are enabled to be genuinely alone, for the fear of obscurity is gone; and we are enabled to be genuinely with others, for they no longer control us.

It is not difficult to see how dependent simplicity is upon solitude. Enslavement to the opinions of others is the source of a great deal of duplicity in modern society. How often we discover our action to be prompted, not by the divine Center, but by what others may say or think. Sadly, we must confess that our experience is all too frequently characterized by endless attempts to justify what we do or fail to do. And how violently this problem rears its ugly head the moment we seek a simpler lifestyle. Whereas before we were tyrannized by the desire to look affluent, now we are tyrannized by the desire to look scant. If what we own can look slightly austere and unvarnished, then perhaps others will think we live in simplicity. Painfully, we know we are too dependent upon the approval of others. We sincerely want to do what is right, but our own self-consciousness betrays our lack of true simplicity. Our struggle affirms the observation of François Fénelon, "These people are sincere, but they are not simple."[6] The grace of solitude must be rooted deep within if we are to know simplicity of heart.

And so it is with all the Christian Disciplines. If we detach simplicity from them, we will turn it into something other than what it is. But when we view it within the landscape of the whole of Christian spirituality, we gain balance and perspective.

It is not wrong for us to isolate some aspect of the spiritual walk for the sake of study, as long as we understand the artificiality of the isolation. And we must always come back to the whole. Perhaps the technical sciences can ignore the whole for the part,* but in the spiritual walk it is ruinous. The life with God, hid in Christ, is a unity, a seamless robe. That, of course, is the essence of its simplicity and the cause of its complexity.

We might be tempted to discouragement by the apparent intricacies of a subject we thought would be straightforward and easy to grasp. At times simplicity seems as elusive as humility; the moment we think we have it we have lost it. It seems fraught with hidden crevices and box canyons. How can we ever expect to pick our way through these perplexing catacombs?

If, in a small way, this describes your feelings and fears and even frustrations, I would like to bring you a word of encouragement. The very sense of awe you feel at the immensity of the task is the first requirement for entering the grace of simplicity. Those who come bolting in discover not simplicity, but arrogance.

Beyond that, you will be encouraged to discover that simplicity is much more tangled in analysis than it is in practice. If you desire Christ and his way with sincerity of heart, he will faithfully teach you. He will not let you stray far. Lovingly, tenderly, he will always bring you back to the straight gate and the narrow way. You need not worry if you find it difficult to ex-

---

* This is called specializing, and I have my reservations about it even in the technical sciences.

plain exactly what this virtue is. We could well say of simplicity what Thomas à Kempis said of compunction of heart, "It is better to practice it than to know how to define it."[7]

Models of simplicity are desperately needed today. Our task is urgent and relevant. Our century thirsts for the authenticity of simplicity, the spirit of prayer, and the life of obedience. May we be the embodiment of that kind of authentic living.

2. THE BIBLICAL ROOTS: THE OLD COVENANT

All plenty which is not my God is poverty to me.
—St. Augustine

Simplicity is deeply rooted in the Old Testament revelation. In it, God revealed both what he is like and how people are to live. The two ideas are inseparable. The more clearly we understand the nature of God, the more clearly we understand how we are to live.

The pressing question today is not, "Is there a God?" but, "What kind of God is there?" Few seriously champion atheism because of its obvious intellectual vulnerability, but many have searching questions about what God is like. Is God cruel or is he good? In short, can God be trusted? Simplicity of heart can flourish only in the fertile soil of trust, and it is the Old Testament's revelation of the faithfulness and goodness of God that opens the door to that trust.

We also struggle to understand how we are to live. Few of us would buy into the naive notion that the accumulation of bigger and better things will give us joy or purpose. Yet neither are we comfortable with the rigid ascetic who thunders down denunciations on the evil of possessions. We don't want to be materialists, ever acquiring and ever hoarding. And yet, John the Baptist with his skins and wild honey doesn't quite seem the model either. How can we put material things in a proper perspective in a world of dental bills and piano lessons? How do we decide for or against a new microwave oven or a dishwasher? This ancient record of God's revelation to his people, Israel, provides us with important hints for answering such questions.

It is, of course, a long journey from Kadesh-barnea to London or Chicago in both space and time. The cultural distance might tempt us to wonder if instruction about lifestyle—even divine instruction—given to shepherds and farmers would have any relevance to modern urbanites. What does the law of gleaning have to do with the consumer price index? How can the year of Jubilee possibly relate to the international trade deficit?

The problem is a real one, but thoughtful people realize that though specific legislation often has only parochial application, the principles inherent in that legislation are timeless. In fact, the Old Testament revelation provides us with some of the most profound perceptions into life to be found anywhere. That, of course, does not solve the hermeneutical question of how to understand the perceptions, or the practical question of how to apply the perceptions, but it does save us from temporal snobbishness.

Radical Dependence

The creation story is the starting point for our understanding of simplicity. At center stage is God, who speaks, and at his word the entire universe comes crashing into being. The high point of his creative effort is humanity, whom he made male and female.

The radical dependence of the entire creation upon God is a central teaching of this breathtaking narrative, and certainly the pivotal notion for our understanding of simplicity. We have no independent existence, no self-sustaining ability. All we are and all we possess is derived.

We need to lift high the biblical doctrine of creation today, particularly our own creatureliness. We are not the captains of our souls nor the masters of our fates. We are part of the created order and hence totally dependent. Our posture is not one of arrogant acquisition, but of simple trust. What we have or ever will have comes from his gracious hand.

We are dependent upon God for even our sense of worth as individuals. Our uniqueness and dignity is rooted in our creation in the image of God. Our value is not tied to wealth, status, accomplishments, or position. It is a gift. Obviously, this wonderful truth flies in the face of the modern tendency to define people by what they produce or what they have.

The terrible reality of the fall was nothing more than a repudiation of our dependence upon God. Adam and Even took to themselves what God had forbidden. They said, in effect, "We will provide for ourselves." They mistrusted the goodness of God by believing the serpent's lie that God was holding back from them something good. And when they did, they realized that they were naked. The nakedness in question was not so much a lack of clothes as it was the awful vulnerability which they assumed in repudiating their dependence. Independence always comes at a high price, and especially so when it involves a rejection of the gracious provision of God.

Simplicity means a return to the posture of dependence. Like children we live in a spirit of trust. What we have we receive as a gift.

Radical Obedience

If the first insight into simplicity that we receive from the Old Testament is radical dependence, the second is radical obedience. Perhaps nowhere is this more graphically seen than when Abraham was called upon to surrender his most priceless treasure—his son Isaac. God spoke, Abraham obeyed. No contingency plans, no skirting around the issue, no ifs ands or buts. Through a long painful process Abraham's life had been honed down to one truth—obedience to the voice of Yahweh. This "holy obedience" forms the grid through which the life of simplicity flows.

Radical obedience is possible only when God has our supreme allegiance. The Ten Commandments begin with three staccato warnings against idolatry. Idolatry is, of course, the attempt to erect an allegiance higher than God. "No," shouts the Decalogue; the one true God must be the heart of our devotion.

Today we need to hear again that God alone is worthy of our worship and obedience. The idolatry of affluence is rampant. Our greed for more dictates so many of our decisions. Notice how the fourth commandment of the Sabbath rest strikes at the heart of this everlasting itch to get ahead. We find it so very hard to rest when, by working, we can get the jump on everyone else. There is no greater need today than the freedom to lay down the heavy burden of getting ahead.

The prohibition against covetousness is the tenth commandment. At the heart of the sin of covetousness is the inner lust to have. Obviously, there is nothing wrong with having things; it is the inordinate desire, the inner compulsion, the undisciplined craving that is condemned. Covetousness is the idolatrous worship of things. But, and here comes the rub, all of us feel that we are in complete control of our desire for things. We would never admit to an ungovernable spirit of covetousness. The problem is that we, like the alcoholic, are unable to recognize the disease once we have been engulfed by it. Only by the help of others are we able to detect the inner spirit that places wealth above God. And we must come to fear the idolatrous state of covetousness because the moment things have priority, radical obedience becomes impossible.

The Generosity of God

A dominant note in the Old Testament witness is the generosity of God, who freely gives to his children. Repeatedly in the creation story we have the confession that the earth is good. God lavished abundant provision upon the original pair.

God called Abram from Ur of the Chaldeans to be the father of a new nation. With that call was the promise to make Abram's name great and to prosper him in material ways (Gen. 12:1–7). This pledge was certainly fulfilled, for we are informed that "Abram was very rich in cattle, in silver, and in gold" (Gen. 13:2).

Abraham's son of promise, Isaac, was likewise showered with material provision: "The Lord blessed him [Isaac], and the man became rich, and gained more and more until he became very wealthy. He had possessions of flocks and herds, and a great household, so that the Philistines envied him" (Gen. 26:12–14). Even Jacob, who received the parental blessing through deceit, was indeed blessed. When he sought to return to his homeland he offered to Esau, his brother, a tribute that only the genuinely wealthy could afford—490 costly animals, including thirty camels with their young (Gen. 32:13–21). Joseph and Job both went through the crucible of obedience and both were rewarded handsomely in the end. Solomon chose wisdom above wealth, but received both in abundance.

The book of Deuteronomy is peppered throughout with promised blessing, and we do the text a grave injustice if we seek to spiritualize the blessing. It was literal land and flocks with which God said he would bless the people: "He will love you, bless you, and multiply you; he will also bless the fruit of your body and the fruit of your ground, your grain and your wine and your oil, the increase of your cattle and the young of your flock" (Deut. 7:13). Deuteronomy 16:15 is typical of so much in this echoed law code: "God will bless you in all your produce and in all the work of your hands, so that you will be altogether joyful." Note that the rejoicing is *because* of the abundant provision from the hand of God.

Even the Book of Amos, which lashed out so viciously at the uncompassionate accumulation of wealth, saw a day:

> When the plowman shall overtake the reaper
> and the treader of grapes him who sows the seed;
> the mountains shall drip sweet wine,
> and all the hills shall flow with it.
> I will restore the fortunes of my people Israel . . .
> says the Lord your God. (Amos 9:13–15)

And Malachi flatly declared that, if only the people would open their hearts in obedient giving, God would open the windows of heaven and pour out upon them material blessing beyond what they could possibly contain (Mal. 3:10).

We do need to stress that the promise of material blessing was a conditioned promise. It was no blank check. There was the stipulation, "If you are willing and obedient you shall eat the good of the land" (Isa. 1:19). That is to say, there was the strong emphasis upon the inward nature of simplicity—holy obedience—that conditioned all the promised provision. And a vital aspect of that obedience was compassionate provision for the poor and needy.

And why shouldn't the high note of obedience have among its secondary notes the promise of blessing? After all, it would be a strange kind of God who would always repay obedience by withholding the good of the earth. Such did sometimes happen, as the Psalmist testified, but even so he was puzzled by the prosperity the wicked enjoyed while he suffered (Ps. 73). God at times does withhold material blessing for our greater good, but that is the exception to the rule of gracious provision, which is also for our good. It is like God to want to give us good things.

The connection between obedience and blessing is genuinely significant, and the significance is not primarily in the notion of being rewarded for doing what is right. That has its place, but it is a minor place, almost a childish place. *The deeper reality in obedience is the kind of spirit it works into us.* It is a spirit that crucifies greed and covetousness. It is a spirit of compassion and outreach. It is a spirit of sensitivity and trust. Once this inner disposition has taken over our personality, material blessings cannot hurt us, for they *will* be used for right purposes. We will recognize material goods to be not for us alone, but for the good of all.

This leads to another important factor in understanding the Old Testament emphasis upon material blessings. Almost without exception the promised provision was for the community rather than the individual. The stress was upon the good of the nation, the tribe, the clan. The idea that one could cut off a piece of the consumer pie and go off and enjoy it in isolation was unthinkable.

Generosity Begets Generosity

God's great generosity to us sets us free to model that generosity toward others. Because he gave, we are enabled to give.

This celebration of the generosity of God and freedom to give in return is clearly seen in the year of Jubilee (Lev. 25). The Jubilee was a call to a divinely enabled freedom from possessions and an equitable restructuring of social arrangements.

Once every fifty years, on the Day of Atonement, the loud trumpet was to sound proclaiming "liberty throughout the land to all its inhabitants" (Lev. 25:10). All slaves were to be set free. All debts were to be canceled. All land was to be returned to the original owner.

Inherent in the concept of the Jubilee was a carefree spirit of joyous trust. God could be relied upon to provide what was needed. He had promised, "I will command my blessing upon you" (Lev. 25:21). It was this inner spirit of trust that gave the ability to meet the stipulations of the Jubilee.

There was an important social principle in the Jubilee. If faithfully executed (which it was not), it would have utterly eliminated the age-old problem of the rich becoming richer and the poor becoming poorer. It was, in effect, legislative justice on behalf of the poor; an institutionalized legal mechanism for solving a social and spiritual problem. The vicious cycle of poverty could be broken. Parents who had lost everything and were forced to sell themselves into slavery to survive knew that their children need not be crushed with their economic legacy. They could have a fresh start. Conversely, the wealthy could not forever lord it over those less fortunate. Their advantaged position was not perpetual.

We would do well today to take a thoughtful look at this unique approach for curbing social injustice. We live in a world in which the gulf that separates the haves and the have-nots is widening at a phenomenal rate. It is, of course, the height of simplistic thinking to assume that you can take an ancient and local law and attempt to universalize it and apply it to the complex international scene. But neither is the Jubilee principle totally irrelevant to our day. In fact, it just might give us some important clues into ways we could have a saner, more just world.

Another interesting thing about the Jubilee was the perspective it gave on the land, a perspective that was characteristic of Old Testament thought. The land did not have value in and of itself, but only in terms of the number of crops it would produce until the Jubilee (Lev. 26:16). Land was not used as an investment as is common today. The point was that the children of Israel did not own the land; they were merely given the use of it. God was the sovereign of the land: "The land shall not be sold in perpetuity, for the land is mine" (Lev. 25:23). Like the treasurer of a company or the housekeeper of a mansion, human authority over the land was one of supervision. God had so parceled out the land that all the people could benefit from its produce.

This principle of equitable distribution rather than hoarding, and managership rather than ownership, was as revolutionary then as it is now. What would happen if this idea—that the purpose of the land is to serve the needs of humanity rather than provide the means of self-aggrandizement—were to be accepted today? What would that say to our real estate investments? Perhaps such an approach would not meet with general approval, but what if Christians were to believe that the land was for the good of all people alike? Is it possible that this group alone could unleash resources that would amputate starvation from the face of the earth?

We have no historical evidence that the children of the covenant ever implemented the Jubilee. However, that tells us only that they were often a stiff-necked and disobedient people; it provides no light on the rightness or workability or even desirability of such an arrangement. What the Jubilee principle does show us is God's deep abiding concern for justice and equity.

The law of the first fruits also illustrates how our generosity flows out of God's generosity. This law stipulated that the first of the crop to ripen was to be given to God. It was, in effect, an act of trust in the generosity of God. They gave in confidence that they would be able to bring in the rest of the harvest. It was an acted-out confession of God as the gracious Giver of all good things.

Similar to the law of first fruits, the tithe was a concept of joyful celebration. By Jesus' day this delightful rule had become as twisted and abused as it has in our own day. It is sad to think that tithing, which was intended to express liberation and freedom, has been so often turned into another way to put people into bondage.

The custom of tithing is first mentioned in the Bible in connection with Abraham. Upon his return from a retaliation raid, Abraham joyfully gave Melchizedek a tenth of the spoils and gave 100 percent of the remainder to the King of Sodom. Although the King objected, Abraham insisted, "Lest you should say, 'I have made Abram rich'" (Gen. 14:17–24). Abraham gave lavishly in celebration of God's power over his enemies. He was not counting each shekel to ensure his fair share—he wanted to get rid of it all. There was a spirit of joy and freedom connected with the giving.

The Mosaic law maintains this sense of joyful festivity. A full tenth of the Israelite's income, beyond the first fruits, was to be given away in celebration of the gracious provision of God. The money was used to care for the Levites, the sojourner, and the poor and needy. It was also used to underwrite the expenses of the festivities involved in celebrating God's generosity:

> You shall tithe all the yield of your seed . . . and before the Lord your God . . . you shall eat the tithe of your grain, of your wine, and of your oil, and the firstlings of your herd and flock; that you may learn to fear the Lord your God always . . . and spend the money for whatever you desire, oxen, or sheep, or wine, or strong drink, whatever your appetite craves; and you shall eat there before the Lord your God and rejoice, you and your household. And you shall not forsake the Levite who is within your towns, for he has no portion or inheritance with you. (Deut. 14:22–27)

In effect, this amounted to an all-expense-paid religious holiday. Tithe money used for a glorious holy party! At the heart of the tithe was a joyous spirit of generosity, worship, celebration.

Nor is that all. In the regulations regarding the tithe we can see God's special concern for the helpless and the needy, which is always an important ingredient in simplicity. Every third year the tithe money was to be gathered together and used specifically for those who were unable to care for themselves. "At the end of every three years you shall bring forth all the tithe . . . and the Levite . . . the sojourner, the fatherless, and the widow . . . shall come and eat and be filled" (Deut. 14:28–29). In an agrarian society, land was the principal means of support, and so the Levite and the sojourner stood outside the normal means of earning a living. In a patriarchal culture the fatherless and the widows also stood outside the ordinary means of support. Given the make up of Jewish culture in that period, these four groups of people were the least able to care for themselves. And because of God's compassionate concern for them, this provision was written into the tithe.

We would do well to consider, given the shape of modern society, whether there are people today that parallel the Levites, the sojourners, the fatherless, and the widows. By the very nature of our culture, are there groups that are left outside the normal means of self-supporting income? If so, do not the rest of us have an obligation to respond to their need?

It should be noted that the New Testament does not make use of either the tithe or the first fruits. Jesus had a great many things to say about our attitude toward possessions but he mentions the tithe only twice, in both cases negatively (Luke 18:21, Matt. 23:22). The Apostle Paul had a good deal to say about giving, but any reference to the law of the tithe is conspicuously absent. Neither Jesus nor Paul ever made the tithe the basis for Christian stewardship. The reason for this will be discovered in Chapter 3.

Perhaps the patriarch Abraham should be the paradigm for our understanding of the principle of generosity. Here was a man who was given great wealth. However, it was never a wealth to be hoarded; rather, it was freely shared with the clan. Indeed, Abraham exhibited an unusual posture of relaxed nonchalance toward possessions. When the covetous spirit of Lot brought them into conflict, Abraham literally gave him the pick of the land (Gen. 13:5-12). Freely he received, freely he gave.

The Call for Justice

The call for justice is one of the great themes that echoes throughout the Old Covenant. We gain insight into this cry for justice through the Hebrew word *mishpat* (מִשְׁפָּט). This was a frequently used word, rich in meaning; a legal term that also carried ethical and religious connotations. *Mishpat* involved a morality over and above strict legal justice; it included observance of good custom or established practice, especially the practice of an equitable distribution of the land. It was used so constantly in conjunction with the Hebrew word for righteousness that the biblical scholar Volkmar Herntrich believes the two concepts should be viewed as virtually synonymous.[1] This is vividly seen in the impassioned plea of Amos, "Let justice roll down like waters, and righteousness like an everflowing stream" (Amos 5:24).

In Deuteronomy we are told that Yahweh "executes justice for the fatherless and the widow, and loves the sojourner, giving him food and clothing" (Deut. 10:18). And again the Psalmist declares, "The Lord works vindication and justice for all who are oppressed" (Ps. 103:6).

This justice involved the wisdom to bring equitable, harmonious relationships between people. Solomon prayed to receive wisdom to govern the people and God responded, "You have asked for yourself understanding to discern what is right [mishpat]" (I Kings 3: 11).

Political leaders were to exercise this quality of ethical compassion on behalf of all people. Micah accuses the rulers of Israel of economic cannibalism for their brutal injustice. They "eat the flesh of my people" and "chop them up like meat in a kettle," laments Micah (Micah 3:1–3). Jeremiah was brokenhearted that justice could not be found anywhere in Jerusalem, though a person would search every street (Jer. 1:5).

There were repeated warnings against the failure to provide justice: "Cursed be he who perverts the justice due to the sojourner, the fatherless, and the widow" (Deut. 27:19).* Great was the blessing promised to those who did exercise justice: "Happy is he . . . who executes justice for the oppressed; who gives food to the hungry" (Ps. 146:7).

The prophets spared no quarter in denouncing the blatant failure of the people to do justice. The scathing denunciations of Amos are legion. Echoing throughout the book is the charge that "They sell the righteous for silver, and the needy for a pair of shoes" (Amos 2:6). He charges that the women "oppress the poor" and "crush the needy" in their lust for an ever higher standard of living (Amos 4:1). The people were so filled with

---

* Also note Exodus 23:6; Deuteronomy 24:17; Job 36:6; Isaiah 10:2; Jeremiah 5:28.

greed that they could hardly wait for the end of the Sabbath so that they could "make the ephah small and shekel great, and deal deceitfully with false balances (Amos 8:4–6). Bribery was the order of the day, and just judges who spoke the truth were despised (Amos 5:10, 12). Is it any wonder that Amos cried out, "Let justice roll down like waters, and righteousness like an everflowing stream" (Amos 5:24)?

While Amos was lashing out against Israel in the north, Isaiah, in the southern kingdom, lamented, "Everyone loves a bribe and runs after gifts" (Isa. 1:23). Isaiah depicts a courtroom scene in which God is the prosecuting attorney who exposes the unjust practices of the rulers: "What do you mean by crushing my people, by grinding the face of the poor?" (Isa. 3:13–15).

Judah's oppression had extended all the way to official decrees and law books. Just as God had institutionalized a system of compassionate justice, the rulers had institutionalized a system of hardened injustice: "Woe to those who decree iniquitous decrees, and the writers who keep writing oppression" (Isa. 10:1–2). We are told that God abhorred all of Judah's pious rituals because they lacked social relevance. The life pleasing to God is not found in a series of religious duties but in obedience. The fast that God desired was for the people to "loose the bonds of wickedness" and to "let the oppressed go free." God's words to them were these: "Share your bread with the hungry" and bring the "homeless poor into your house" (Isa. 58:5–7).

Among the prophets there was no more plaintive or heartfelt cry than the voice of Jeremiah. He was called the weeping prophet, and with good reason. How he loved the great city of Jerusalem. He agonized over the sin of her people, he pled with them to repent. How broken-hearted he was when his own prophecies of destruction were fulfilled. He is a sad, yet faithful figure in desperate times.

Like the others before him, Jeremiah called the people back to the ancient covenant with its stipulation to "do justice and righteousness, and deliver from the hand of the oppressor him who has been robbed" (Jer. 22:3). Repeatedly he called them to plead the "cause of the fatherless," and to "defend the rights of the needy" (Jer. 5:28, 22:15). But sadly he had to admit, "You have eyes and heart only for your dishonest gain, for shedding innocent blood, and for practicing oppression and violence" (Jer. 22:17).

The tragedy was that the Exile could have been avoided if the people had turned in repentance to God: "If you truly execute justice one with another . . . then I will let you dwell in this place, in the land that I gave of old to your fathers forever" (Jer. 7:5–7). But the Exile did occur and the tragedy of it echoes through the centuries. Injustice, intertwined with idolatry, forced God to send Israel into captivity.

The Call for Compassion

The theme of compassion weaves its way throughout the Old Testament and can be vividly seen in the theologically rich word *hesed* (חֶסֶד). *Hesed* is so laden with meaning that the translators struggle to find an English equivalent, often rendering it "loving kindness" or "mercy." But *hesed* also carries with it the idea of endurance or faithfulness. It is most frequently used in reference to God's unwavering compassion for his people. His wonderful *hesed* is from everlasting to everlasting (Ps. 103:17). It endures forever (Ps. 106:1). It was this quality of limitless mercy which God revealed to Moses when he had asked to see God's glory: "The Lord passed before him, and proclaimed, 'The Lord, the Lord, a God merciful and gracious, slow to anger, and abounding in steadfast love [*hesed*] and faithfulness, keeping steadfast love [*hesed*] for thousands, forgiving iniquity and transgression and sin' " (Exod. 34:6–7).

However (and here is the great challenge), this covenant love, this durable mercy, which is so central to the character of God, is to be reflected in our lives as well. God declares through Hosea the prophet, "I desire steadfast love [*hesed*] and not sacrifice, the knowledge of God, rather than burnt offerings" (Hos. 6:6). And the wisdom of Proverbs counsels, "He who pursues righteousness and kindness [*hesed*] will find life and honor" (Prov. 21:21).

But most amazing of all is the way in which the biblical writers bring together the justice of *mishpat* and the compassion of *hesed*. To give people what is due them is one thing; the quality of spirit through which we relate to them is quite another. Zechariah received this mighty word of the Lord, "Thus says the Lord of hosts, Render true judgments [mishpat], show kindness and mercy [hesed] each to his brother, do not oppress the widow, the fatherless, the sojourner, or the poor; and let none of you devise evil against his brother in your heart" (Zech. 7:9–10). In his call to repentance, Hosea tenderly pled with the people, "So you, by the help of God, return, hold fast to love [hesed] and justice [mishpat], and wait continually for your God" (Hos. 12:6). And in what must be considered one of the most insightful summations of our task in all the Old Testament, we have again the outward demand of justice combined with the inward spirit of compassion:

> He has showed you, O man, what is good:
>   and what does the Lord require of you
> but to do justice [mishpat], and to love kindness [hesed],
>   and to walk humbly with your God? (Mic. 6:8)

Compassion and justice blended call us to simplicity of life.

Sprinkled throughout the Old Covenant is what I call its laws of compassion and concern. Perhaps the one most quickly recognized is the law of gleaning (Lev. 19:9–20; 23:22, Deut. 24:19–20). In harvesting, the farmer was to leave some of the crop along the borders and the grain which fell as he worked, so that the poor could gather it. "And when you reap the harvest of your land, you shall not reap your field to its very border, nor shall you gather the gleanings after your harvest; you shall leave them for the poor and for the stranger: I am the Lord your God" (Lev. 23:22). Likewise, the vineyards and the olive groves were not to be stripped bare so that there could be provision for the needy. The book of Ruth gives a vivid portrayal of the tenderness in this law. Naomi and her daughter-in-law, Ruth, had returned to Israel husbandless and landless and hence helpless, but they were able to gather the gleanings from the field of Boaz (Ruth 2:1 ff.).

At the heart of God is compassionate concern for the broken and desperate. By means of the law of gleaning, he placed into the economy of Israel provision for those who, for whatever reason, had become disadvantaged. There seemed to be an almost holy indifference about whether or not the person deserved to be poor; the simple fact that the person was without was sufficient reason to provide for his or her need.

Consider the tenderness in the old laws of giving and taking a pledge. If a neighbor borrowed your oxcart and left his coat in pledge, you had to be sure to give the coat back before sunset, even if he hadn't finished with the oxcart. Why? Because the night air was cold and he needed the coat for warmth. If you refused and your neighbor cried out to God in the chilly night, God warned, "I will hear, for I am compassionate" (Exod. 22:26–27). Deuteronomy made this rule especially binding if the pledge had been given by a poor person, since in all likelihood he had no other coat with which to keep warm (Deut. 24:12). A widow's coat could not be taken as a pledge—she was helpless enough as it was (Deut. 24–17). A millstone could not be taken as a pledge—it was a man's livelihood (Deut. 24:6). It was forbidden to barge into a neighbor's house to get a pledge; you were to wait at the front door until he brought it out (Deut. 24:10–11). Graciousness and common courtesy were to penetrate all human relationships, even business dealings.

Note the approach to the giving of loans. Since it was assumed that debtors would be among the poor and vulnerable, the charging of interest on loans was forbidden. It was viewed as an unbrotherly exploitation of another's misfortune and only served to deepen his dependency (Deut. 23:19).

Wages were to be paid to the poor on the day the work was done, undoubtedly because the money would be needed for supper (Deut. 24:14–15). If you were hungry you could eat from your neighbor's vineyard or grainfield, but you were not allowed to put any in a bucket (Deut. 23:24). And on it goes. Tender commands. Wise empathetic instruction on interpersonal relationships.

This quality of compassion and concern extended even to the animals and the land. We often forget that the Sabbath rest principle included the needs of the livestock: "Six days you shall do your work, but on the seventh day you shall rest; that your ox and your ass may have rest" (Exod. 23:12). The land itself needed "a year of solemn rest" (Lev. 25:5). Every seventh year there was to be no planting and no harvesting, for "the land shall keep a sabbath to the Lord" (Lev. 25:2). Even the soil of the vineyards was not to be overtaxed by planting other crops between the rows (Deut. 22:9). The oxen that trod out the grain should not be muzzled in order to allow them to eat while they worked (Deut. 25:4). Baby birds might be taken, but the mother bird must be left to care for remaining eggs and to produce future young (Deut. 22:6–7).

The whole point of this instruction is that our dominion over the earth and the little creatures that creep upon it is to be a compassionate dominion. We are not to rape the earth but to care for it—kindly, lovingly, tenderly.

These old laws, regulations, and moral judgments temper and tender our aggressiveness. Like the mysterious manna from heaven, there is always enough to care for one's needs, but never any for hoarding. There is a limit to a good thing, and whenever that limit is transgressed a good thing turns into a bad thing. Our task is to bring things into their God-ordained perspective, and these Old Testament laws give us intriguing hints at what that perspective should be.

The Call for Wholeness

The vision for wholeness and peace, which shines like a beacon of light through the Old Covenant, gives us important insights into Christian simplicity. This theme is wonderfully gathered up in the Hebrew word *shalom,* שָׁלוֹם,[2] a full-bodied concept that resonates with wholeness, unity, balance. Gathering in (but much broader than) peace, it means a harmonious, caring community with God at its center as the prime sustainer and most glorious inhabitant. This great vision of *shalom* begins and ends our Bible. In the creation narrative, God brought order and harmony out of chaos; in the Apocalypse of John, we have the glorious wholeness of a new heaven and a new earth. The messianic child to be born is to be the Prince of Peace (Isa. 9:6). Justice and righteousness and peace are to characterize his unending kingdom (Isa. 9:7). Central to the dream of *shalom* is the wonderful vision of all nations streaming to the mountain of the temple of God to be taught his ways and to walk in his paths; to beat their swords into plowshares and their spears into pruning hooks (Isa. 2:2–5; Mic. 4:1–4). *Shalom* even carries the idea of a harmonious unity in the natural order: the cow and the bear become friends, the lion and the lamb lie down together, and a little child leads them (Isa. 11:1–9). We are in harmony with God—faithfulness and loyalty prevail. We are in harmony with our neighbor—justice and mercy abound. We are in harmony with nature—peace and unity reign.

Economically and socially, the vision of *shalom* is captured in what Bishop John Taylor calls "The Theology of Enough." The greed of the rich is tempered by the need of the poor. Justice, harmony, equilibrium prevail. "It meant a dancing kind of inter-relationship, seeking something more free than equality, more generous than equity, the ever-shifting equipoise of a life-system."[3] Excessive extravagance, vaunting ambition, ravaging greed—all are foreign to the complete contented brotherhood of *shalom*. Under the reign of God's *shalom* the poor are no onger oppressed, because covetousness no longer rules.

In a particularly tender scene, Jeremiah lamented the fraud and greed of prophet and priest, saying, "They have healed the wound of my people lightly, saying, 'Peace, peace,' when there is no peace" (Jer. 6:14). In essence, Jeremiah had filed a malpractice suit against the self-styled religious quacks. They had put a Band-Aid over a gaping social wound and said, "*Shalom, shalom*—all will be well." But Jeremiah thundered, in effect, "*En shalom*—all is not well. Justice is spurned, the poor oppressed, the orphan ignored. There is no wholeness or healing here!"

But the healing peace of God will not be spurned forever. Isaiah saw a day when the reconcilation between people will be a reality, a day when justice and righteousness will reign, a time when the wholeness of God's peace will rule and people will "walk in the light of the Lord" (Isa. 2:4–5).

In an especially poignant passage, Scripture brings together the three Hebrew concepts we have studied: justice, compassion, and peace. The Psalmist points to the day when "Steadfast love and faithfulness will meet; righteousness and peace will kiss each other" (Ps. 85:10).

What is God's word for the world in which we live? Does he

see justice and righteousness increasing among us? Is he saddened by our lack of compassion? Are there any who embrace his peace as a way of life?

I am not posing these questions only to the world at large. I query us who own Christ as our life. Can God be pleased by the vast and increasing inequities among us? Is he not grieved by our arrogant accumulation, while Christian brothers and sisters elsewhere languish and die? Is it not obligatory upon us to see beyond the nose of our own national interest, so that justice may roll down like waters and righteousness like an everflowing stream? Is there not an obligation upon us to do justice, and to love mercy, and to walk humbly with God if we want to live in his wonderful peace?

These are tough questions, I know. But they are questions we must ask if we are to take seriously God's word to us through the Old Covenant.

3. THE BIBLICAL ROOTS: THE NEW COVENANT

I place no value on anything I possess, except in relation to the Kingdom of God.
                                        —David Livingstone

In his manifesto on the poor, Jesus declares his intention to "set at liberty those who are oppressed" (Luke 4:18). And as he went among people teaching and healing, he observed the many oppressions that bore down upon them. He sought to lift their burdens, and as he did he spoke repeatedly and vigorously of one of the greatest burdens they bore—the burden of providing for themselves against tomorrow.

He saw how people were broken by the effort to attain riches. He perceived their awful vulnerability in believing that it was their responsibility to provide for themselves, to watch out for number one. The Apostle Paul said that those who desire wealth have "pierced their hearts with many pangs" (I Tim. 6:9-10). And Jesus observed the pangs that had pierced the hearts of so many, the pangs of striving for riches.

Jesus also saw how people were crushed by the failure to obtain riches. In his day it was considered a mark of God's displeasure to be poor. And those who had failed to receive the goods of this world could not help feeling that somehow God was against them. Remember how baffled the disciples were when Jesus told them that a camel could slip through the eye of a needle more easily than the wealthy could enter the Kingdom of God (Matt. 19:24)? This astonishment was due primarily to their belief that the wealth of the rich young ruler was a sign of God's special favor upon him. No wonder they exclaimed, "Who then can be saved?" (Matt. 19:25). And Jesus perceived how bruised and trampled in spirit people were because they were poor and felt God was displeased with them. Repeatedly he opposed this false and destructive doctrine, showing instead that in the economy of God, the poor, the broken, the halt were special objects of his blessing and concern (Matt. 5:1-12). By word and deed he sought to lift the burden of the discouraged and disheartened.

Jesus further saw the wearisome burden upon those who had gotten riches and were trying to hold onto them. He knew the cancerous nature of wealth and often warned of its dangers. He spoke of the "deceitfulness of riches" (Matt. 13:22, KJV). Riches are deceitful precisely because they lead us to trust in them, and Jesus saw that trap and the spiritual destructiveness which attends it. This was the burden that bore down upon the rich young ruler. Not only did he have great possessions, but more significantly, the great possessions had him. Of all oppressions his was the most spiritually debilitating.

To all those weighted down by the burden of tomorrow, or any other burden, Jesus extends a gracious invitation, "Come to me, all who labor and are heavy laden, and I will give you rest. Take my yoke upon you, and learn from me; for I am gentle and lowly in heart, and you will find rest for your souls. For my yoke is easy, and my burden is light" (Matt. 11:28-30). Our task in the pages that follow is to seek an understanding of the teaching which undergirds this call to liberation, this summons to simplicity of life.

Christ the Center

The most radiant passage on Christian simplicity in all the Bible must be Matthew 6.[1] It simply sparkles with joy and trust. Earlier, Jesus announced that the Kingdom of God has burst upon the human scene. Hence we can live in a new glorious inner liberty in alms giving, praying, and fasting without any need for human approval. We can obey the trenchant command, "Do not lay up for yourselves treasures on earth" (Matt. 6:19). We can live lives focused upon stockpiling "treasures in heaven" (Matt. 6:20). We can be scandalously free from anxiety, because we are under the watchful eye of him who richly cares for the birds of the air and the lilies of the field. No longer do we need to bear on our backs the soul-crushing gentile burden of the world of tomorrow. With focused eye and centered heart we can freely "seek first his Kingdom and his righteousness," knowing that all things needful will be provided (Matt. 6:33).

Jesus teaches us with a negative and a positive command: "Do not lay up for yourselves treasures on earth," but "do lay up for yourselves treasures in heaven" (Matt. 6:19). The "treasures" in view here are not just great riches, but all those things that we trust in and cling to. My boys, for example, have some very special treasures. When I begin to look into what they are, I am frequently amazed, for they may be only some shiny stones, or an odd looking stick, or a pile of rubber bands. But for my children these are coveted treasures. Jesus is warning us that, no matter what our earthly treasures may be, we have to be very careful about holding too tightly to them because they are bound to disappoint us and to keep us from living in the Kingdom of God in the freedom and power we desire. He knows that we have an almost compulsive need to secure ourselves by means of earthly things, but tells us not to do that, and proceeds to give three reasons why we should not amass earthly treasure but should store up heavenly treasure.

The first reason is that this world is a very uncertain place (Matt. 6:19–20). There simply is "no hidin' place down here." Now, today we may not have a problem with moths and rust corrupting our treasure, but it is certainly difficult to find a situation where inflation does not "break in and steal" it. Jesus is forcing us to see that, regardless of how secure our treasure may be, it will ultimately fail us.

The second reason Jesus points to is the fact that whatever we fix as our treasure will obsess our whole life: "For where your treasure is there will your heart be also" (Matt. 6:21). He was not saying that the heart should or should not be where the treasure is, but that it *will* be.

There is no option in this matter: our whole mind will be fixed around our treasure. When Jesus said that "no one can serve two masters," he did not mean that it was unwise to serve two masters, but that it was impossible. If our treasure is in our bank account, or an educational diploma, or any other earthly thing, our mind will not be on God.

Jesus illustrates this fact in the most profound way: "The light of the body is the eye: if therefore thine eye be single, thy whole body shall be full of light" (Matt. 6:22, KJV). If all within us is honed down to the single treasure of Christ and his Kingdom, then we are living in the light of simplicity. The ancient term "single eye" (ὁ ὀφθαλμός ἁπλοῦς) has a rich connotation, which our English has difficulty capturing. It refers both to a single aim in life and to a generous unselfish spirit. The two ideas have such a close connection in the Hebrew mind that they can be expressed in a single phrase. Singleness of purpose toward God and generosity of spirit are twins. The single eye is contrasted with the "evil eye," which is a Semitic expression for a covetous nature.[2]

Jesus lived in this singleness of purpose with God so perfectly that he could say without embellishment that he did nothing of his own accord (John 5:19). His words were the words of the Father, his deeds the deeds of the Father. And, astonishingly, he calls us in our small way to enter this unity of purpose. He invites us to the life of the "single eye" through which the entire personality is bathed in light and unity. With our eye focused on Christ the Center, we are to live with glad and generous hearts. This is simplicity.

The third reason Jesus gives for not laying up treasure on earth is that provision has already been made. The birds of the air and the lilies of the field all witness to an order in the Kingdom of God, in which adequate provision is made for everyone and everything. God provides for us according to our needs, just as he does for the plant and the animal life.

Jesus is not telling us to refrain from making provision. We miss the point of the teaching if, when the family gathers for supper, we announce, "Now, the Bible says to take no thought for supper and so we haven't." No, we work, but we work in faith, not in the anxious concern of distrust. On a practical level it is at this point that the nagging problem of "faith versus works" is resolved. We live centered in trust and faith and all our action and work arises out of that center. It is not fear and anxiety over tomorrow that prompt us to work, but obedience to the divine command. We make provision as it seems right and good (just as the birds do), but what comes to us is not so much the result of our labor as it is the gracious gift of God. We live the carefree life of unconcern for possessions in the midst of our work.

When this spirit of trust pervades all of our efforts, we understand the unwisdom of borrowing evil from tomorrow. No longer distracted by concerns for tomorrow, we seek first Christ's Kingdom and his righteousness. The focus of our thought, speech, and action is Christ the Center.

Identification with the Poor

The life of Christian simplicity is necessarily tied to a concern for the poor and defenseless. We cannot live at the divine Center for long without being compelled to care for our neighbor. For Christ, love of God and love of neighbor were two sides to the same door—we must do both to get through the door. And like the Samaritan, we soon discover that our path often leads to the bleeding and broken of humanity.

Perhaps no book in the New Testament gives a more sustained and passionate plea for the disadvantaged and dispossessed than the Gospel of Luke. Luke is the Gospel of the poor, the voice of the voiceless. Any statistical accounting would demonstrate that Luke gives the most attention to the poor and needy. But beyond sheer scoreboard count, it seems that Luke has a special sensitivity to the hurting and the helpless. This Gospel, then, provides us with a valuable departure point in understanding the New Testament summons to simplicity.

Luke alone records Mary's *Magnificat* with its lovely magnification of the Lord. Its very beauty may cause us to miss its strong advocacy of the lowly and needy:

He has shown strength with his arm,
he has scattered the proud in the imagination of their hearts,
he has put down the mighty from their thrones,
    and exalted those of low degree;
he has filled the hungry with good things,
    and the rich he has sent empty away. (Luke 1:52–53)

The birth story itself is told with stark simplicity: the obedience of Mary, the humility of a manger, the faithfulness of Simeon and Anna. How often we have marveled at God's choosing unpretentious Bethlehem and simple shepherds as the court scene for the regal birth. Perhaps God is teaching us something central about the nature of the Gospel life in the way his only begotten son was born.

Consider the simple counsel John the Baptist gave the common folk: "He who has two coats, let him share with him who has none; and he who has food, let him do likewise." To the tax collectors he urged honesty: "Collect no more than is appointed you." To soldiers he counseled contentment: "Rob no one by violence or by false accusation, and be content with your wages" (Luke 3:11-14). The point of the instruction is its elementary nature—small, simple items that accent the welfare of others.

Again, Luke alone records Jesus' proclamation at Nazareth with its tender advocacy of the poor and oppressed.

The Spirit of the Lord is upon me,
because he has anointed me to preach good news to the poor.
He has sent me to proclaim release to the captives
    and recovering of sight to the blind,
to set at liberty those who are oppressed,
    to proclaim the acceptable year of the Lord. (Luke 4:18-19)

Note the helpless nature of each group—the poor, the captive, the blind, the oppressed. Certainly this shouts to us something of the burden of Jesus Christ. Certainly it must also be the burden of all who follow him.

The beatitudes of Luke are distinguished by their pointed economic perspective: "Blessed are you poor.... Blessed are you that hunger.... Blessed are you that weep.... Woe to you that are rich.... Woe to you that are full.... Woe to you that laugh" (Luke 6:20-21, 24-25). The poor, the hungry, the sad are contrasted with the rich, the full, the happy. It is as if all those classes of people we feel are unblessed and unblessable are showered with special honor. And if that is not enough, those people we would consider to be well off have woes pronounced upon them. Blessings upon the poor, woes upon the rich.

Do these beatitudes mean that God has no concern for the wealthy and self-sufficient? Is God opposed to people of means? The moment we pose the question we sense its absurdity. Deep down we know that God's love is indiscriminate. But how are we to understand these beatitudes? Clearly Jesus was making use of the common Jewish teaching technique of hyperbole to accent God's identification with the weak and the destitute. There is a special divine caring for those who cannot care for themselves. In these beatitudes, Jesus is expressing his burden for the bruised and broken and he invites us to share that burden.

This tenderhearted compassion for the defenseless is again seen in Christ's instructions to his dinner host to invite the poor, the maimed, the lame, and the blind when he gives a banquet (Luke 14:12–14). The purpose of inviting such folk, of course, is not to get one's name in the social register, but because they need help.

Luke's account of the rich man and poor Lazarus underscores the same perspective (Luke 16:19–31). The rich man was not an evil person as we normally think of evil. He had not caused Lazarus' poverty, at least not directly. He did not even chase Lazarus away from his gate as many of us might be tempted to do. He merely ignored him. But that was the great offense! According to Christ, torment in Hades is a just recompense for the failure to respond to the plight of poor Lazarus.

Following a luncheon with Jesus, Zacchaeus exclaimed, "Half of my goods I give to the poor; and if I have defrauded anyone of anything, I restore it fourfold" (Luke 19:8). Honesty, generosity, and concern for the poor belong together. It was this act alone that caused Christ to remark, "Today salvation has come to this house" (Luke 19:9).

The Epistles expressed the same concern. According to the Apostle Paul, the Jerusalem council urged those ministering among the Gentiles to "remember the poor" (Gal. 2:10, but see also Acts 15:35). Former thieves are to learn to labor with their hands in order to "be able to give to those in need" (Eph. 4:28). Even widows are to be characterized by generosity to the afflicted (I Tim. 5:9).

According to the Apostle James, the definition of pure and undefiled religion is "to visit orphans and widows in their affliction, and to keep oneself unstained from the world" (James 1:27). The wealthy are not to receive preferred treatment in the Christian fellowship (James 2:2–9). If a brother or sister is in need, we are to meet that need rather than piously say "Be warmed and filled" (James 2:15). And John, the Apostle of love, reminds us that if we close our hearts to the obvious need of another when we have the ability to help, we do not possess the love of God (I John 3:17).

The Dangers of Wealth

The New Testament consistently and vigorously warns of the dangers of wealth. Many of Jesus' statements on riches and caring for the needy come to us in staccato commands that frighten us. With seemingly reckless abandon, we are advised to "Give to everyone who begs from you; and of him who takes away your goods do not ask them again" (Luke 6:30). And again we are to "Lend, expecting nothing in return" (Luke 6:35). If someone takes our outer cloak we are to surrender our coat as well (Luke 6:29). In terse, pointed language Jesus commands, "Sell your possessions, and give alms" (Luke 12:33). It was not sufficient for the rich young ruler to have an inner spirit of detachment from his possessions; he was commanded literally to sell everything if he wanted the Kingdom of God (Luke 18:22). And with broad strokes the Lord declares, "Whoever of you does not renounce all that he has cannot be my disciple" (Luke 14:33).

If we are shocked by these strong words of Christ and try to retreat from his direct commands to his more general instruction, we find little comfort. To would-be disciples he warned, "Foxes have holes and the birds of the air have nests; but the Son of man has nowhere to lay his head" (Luke 9:58). He told the parable of the rich farmer whose life centered in hoarding, and called him a fool (Luke 12:16–21). He counseled the disciples to travel light: "Take nothing for your journey, no staff, nor bag, nor bread, nor money; and do not have two tunics" (Luke 9:3, but also see Luke 22:36). Jesus said, "Take heed, and beware of all covetousness; for a man's life does not consist in the abundance of his possessions" (Luke 12:15). He declared war on the materialism of his day. The Aramaic term for wealth was "mammon," and Jesus condemned it as a rival god: "You cannot serve God and mammon" (Luke 16:13). Graphically, he depicted the difficulty of the wealthy entering the Kingdom of God to be like a camel attempting to get through the eye of a needle. With God, of course, all things are possible, but Jesus clearly understood the difficulty because he saw the grip that wealth can have on a person.

The Epistles are characterized by the same uncompromising language. Paul declared that "Those who desire to be rich fall into temptation, into a snare, into many senseless and hurtful desires that plunge men into ruin and destruction" (I Tim. 6:9). With embarrassing vigor James denounced the wealthy: "Come now, you rich, weep and howl for the miseries that are coming upon you. Your riches have rotted and your garments are moth-eaten. Your gold and silver have rusted, and their rust will be evidence against you and will eat your flesh like fire" (James 5:1–3). Earlier he had blamed killings and wars on the lust for possessions: "You desire and do not have; so you kill. And you covet and cannot obtain; so you fight and wage war" (James 4:1–2).

Paul said a bishop should not be a "lover of money" (I Tim. 3:8). A deacon should not be "greedy for gain" (I Tim. 3:8). The writer to the Hebrews counseled, "Keep your life free from love of money, and be content with what you have; for he has said, 'I will never fail you nor forsake you'" (Heb. 13:5). Paul called covetousness idolatry and commanded the Corinthian church to exercise stern discipline against anyone guilty of greed (Eph. 5:5, I Cor. 5:11). He listed greed alongside adultery and thievery and declared that those who live in such things would not inherit the Kingdom of God. Paul counseled the wealthy not to trust in their wealth but in God, and to share generously with others (I Tim. 6:17–19). The Spirit had stern words for the lukewarm church in Laodicea which rested in self-sufficient ease: "For you say, I am rich, I have prospered, and I need nothing; not knowing that you are wretched, pitiable, poor, blind, and naked" (Rev. 3:17). Strong, powerful, stringent words indeed!

We sense in these statements an uncompromising and fright-

ening call to discipleship. They are words that do not admit to
"easy Christianity" or "cheap grace," as Bonhoeffer put it. But
this is not the only reason they frighten us (and may I add, just
so that you understand, I too am frightened by this fierce language). These words terrorize us because we read them as laws
that are to be adhered to in every circumstance. Hence we see
no way to limit them. But we simply must understand that the
writers of the New Testament did not intend to give us a new
set of laws. The limit inherent in all these teachings is built
into the simple principle of love of God and neighbor. Dr. Dallas Willard has said, "Love is a well-reasoned concern for the
good of all."[3] Love does not have tunnel vision. If I bring the
needy into my home and destroy my own family in the process,
I am driven by something other than love. These commands of
Jesus must be understood within the broader context of the law
of love. This biblical instruction is not meant to destroy us, but
to set us free. It is the glad trumpet call of liberation to all who
are oppressed by reputation, wealth, and power.

We must not overstate the New Testament criticism of
wealth. Though far from rich, Jesus himself did not come from
the poor masses of Israel. New Testament scholar Martin Hengel surmises that, as a carpenter, Jesus came from "the middle
class of Galilee, the skilled workers."[4] The twelve came from
basically the same background. Zebedee, the father of James
and John, evidently owned the family fishing business, which
employed other laborers beside his sons (Mark 1:20). Matthew
apparently held a rather prestigious position in the tax collect-
ing business before his call by Christ (Mark 2:14). Although
they had left their regular occupations to follow Jesus, the disciples received support from well-to-do women, "who provided
for them out of their means" (Luke 8:3).

Jesus was often among the poor, but he was also frequently
in contact with the rich and privileged. More than once he was
found dining at the banquet table of wealthy Pharisees (Luke
7:36, 11:37, 14:1). Joseph of Arimathea was both a wealthy man
and a disciple of Jesus (Matt. 27:57). Also Nicodemus, who had
come to Jesus at night and later had become a disciple, evidently had considerable means (John 19:39).

Jesus was so far from being a rigid ascetic that he was accused of being a glutton and a drunkard (Luke 7:34). The accusation was obviously a malicious smear, but it pointed to the fact that joyous celebration was an important element in his life. He could rejoice with a young couple in a week-long wedding festival and even provide extra drinks for everyone (John 2:1–11). The Lord could allow the lavish expenditure of perhaps a year's wages to be poured over his head and feet while the disciples grumbled about the needs of the poor (Matt. 26:6–12). The Apostle Paul could rest contented with much as well as little.

What we discover from the New Testament witness is the combination of a penetrating criticism of wealth with a carefree, almost light-hearted attitude toward possessions. It is a combination seldom found today.

The Incendiary Fellowship

When the life and power of the Kingdom of God burst upon the human scene at Pentecost, it was the catalyst for a powerful expression of Christian simplicity. The infant Jerusalem Church is eloquent testimony to that reality. Until then the disciples were a motley crew—bickering, backbiting, jockeying for position, always squabbling over who was to receive top billing. Unfocused, they did not know simplicity of life. But in the course of time Jesus had formed a community of people who would live in holy obedience (always the most distinguishing characteristic of simplicity). Finally a people had been gathered who, when God said, "Wait," would wait, when God said, "Go," would go, when God said, "Give," would give. Rugged men and women who had been seasoned by many failures and some successes, imperfect and ignorant of many things, they were nevertheless a prepared people. And God said, "Wait." Disciplined, obedient, simple, they waited. And the fire fell!

The report of the economic repercussions of that incendiary life burning throughout the fellowship still throbs with joy and freedom: "And all who believed were together and had all things in common; and they sold their possessions and goods and distributed them to all, as any had need" (Acts 2:44-45). The principle was that "as any had need" the others would share of their resources until the need was met.

There was a beautiful, almost unconscious integration of economic sharing with other spiritual disciplines, such as teaching and prayer: "And they devoted themselves to the Apostles' teaching and fellowship, to the breaking of bread and the prayers" (Acts 2:42). Barnabas became something of a paradigm of spontaneous generosity by selling a field to provide for the needs of the fellowship (Acts 4:36-37).

Please remember, we have no indication that what occurred in the early days of the Church was commanded or that it was even the right thing to do. This is not some pattern to be slavishly imitated. What we do see is an incredible freedom to experiment with practical ways to flesh out the meaning of love for God and neighbor. Under the authority of Christ they were freed to try new ways to love one another.

Isn't this the model for us? Not a legal system, but a fresh freedom to discover what it means to live as Christ's disciples together. And the caring we see in Acts gives us significant clues as to which direction the winds of the Spirit desire to blow in our day.

It is important for us to understand the interwoven connection between the fellowship's economic liberality and divine power. In one breath we hear of "wonders and signs" being done by the Apostles, and in the next breath we discover that "All who believed were together and had all things in common" (Acts 2:43-44). We read of the marvelous prayer meeting where the building shook and the people "were all filled with the Holy Spirit and spoke the word of God with boldness" and in the very next verse we discover that "the company of those who believed were of one heart and soul, and no one said that any of the things which he possessed was his own, but they had everything in common" (Acts 4:31-32). As if that were not enough, the very next sentence once again takes up the theme of power: "And with great power the Apostles gave their testimony to the resurrection of the Lord Jesus, and great grace was upon them all" (Acts 4:33). And the next verse echoes their generous sharing. And on it goes, back and forth, interwoven like a tapestry, braided together like a rope.

These passages are not meant to be a systematic theology, and I have no desire to squeeze some kind of normative teaching from them that is universally binding upon the Church. What I am trying to express is that these people were being taken over by the life of the Spirit, which transformed them at every point. They were living on a new level of experience. Signs and wonders and miracles of all kinds abounded. The power of the Holy Spirit was felt and seen. And in the context of that wonderful outpouring of God's life, the sharing of resources was free and generous. And why not? People were being healed, relationships righted, servant leadership exhibited. To be quite honest about it, sharing is not difficult when the power of God is manifest in the midst of his people. His mighty hand and outstretched arm are there to sustain them. Who is there to fear? What better economic security could they have? And if there is ever any instance of deception, as was the case with Ananias and Sapphira, it is cared for quickly through spiritual discernment and the power of God (Acts 5:1–11).

Sometimes people find the joyous sharing of the Jerusalem Church hard to believe. The reason is understandable: they have never seen anything like it in their own experience. But in my small way, and through my limited experience, I want to testify to this reality. When the dynamic presence of God breaks in upon a *sufficiently prepared people,* there is an unguarded sharing that is thrilling, almost frightening. I stress the need for sufficient preparation because, like the early experiences of the disciples, it is possible to know mighty experiences of God's power without it having a lasting impact on the self-centered nature (compare, for example, Luke 9:1 with 9:54). But when a people are gathered who live under the cross and in holy obedience, then the incendiary power of the Holy Spirit can ignite everything, including all economic relationships.

By now you may be wondering, "Why all this talk about miracles, divine power, and spiritual preparation? Can't we just get on with the business of simplifying our lifestyles without all the God talk?" I answer that you are welcome to try, and God help you—because you will sorely need it. Although I deeply empathize with this "holy impatience" to get on with the task, the clear witness of Scripture is that something beyond good intentions and will-power is needed to transform our egocentric, greed-captivated personalities into an all-inclusive community of loving, sharing persons.

There once was a time when I urged simplicity of life upon people indiscriminately. I would cajole, shove, push, and often they would indeed change their lifestyle, but I found that it was all quite destructive. I discovered that simplicity is just another anxiety-laden burden until people have experienced God's gracious power to provide them with daily bread. Only as Kingdom power breaks in are we free to live in trust.

Have you not found it so? Perhaps out of concern for the terrible iniquities in the world, you have sought to open your heart and your pocketbook to needy brothers and sisters. Perhaps you have led the fight for certain causes of compassion in your church and community. You may even have attempted a common purse or some other form of economic sharing. But somehow, deep down inside, it all seems so dry and artificial. There is no oil of the Spirit to heal wounded relationships. Giving is done, but it lacks warmth and vibrancy. Like Moses of old you see the oppression of the people, but also like Moses you have tried the arm of flesh and find it failing you as it did him. For all the good that has been done, you have the uneasy sense that something central is lacking. Could it be that we need to follow the lead of the disciples, who through bitter experience were taught that their first priority was to seek hard after the Kingdom of God, and once baptized into its life and power that they were liberated to care for one another in unprecedented ways?

Freedom to Surrender Our Rights

The attractive ability to surrender our rights for the good of others is central to everything about simplicity. This reality burst forth repeatedly in the experience of the early Christian community. It was based firmly upon the example of Christ who, though rich, for our sakes became poor, and was "obedient to death, even death on a cross" (II Cor. 8:9, Phil. 2.8).

Consider the compassionate manner in which the problem of the neglected Hellenistic widows was resolved (Acts 6:1–7). The Hellenists were Greek-speaking Jews who were quite different culturally from their Hebrew counterparts. Evidently, in the rush of activities, the Greek-speaking widows were overlooked in the daily distribution of food and other goods. No doubt the oversight was completely unintentional, but it produced the potential for a serious split in the infant Church. But under the mighty power of the Spirit it was resolved in the most tender fashion. Wisely, the Apostles refrained from arbitrating the matter and asked that seven be chosen who were filled with the Holy Spirit and wisdom. So tender, so gracious was the spirit of this group that all seven who were chosen were from the aggrieved party—every single one of them had Greek names! The Hebrew believers had given up their own rights. They did not have to have things their own way. They were released from greedy self-serving one-upmanship. And because this freedom from self-interest abounded among them, the widows were cared for, justice prevailed, severed relationships were healed.

How heartening and how instructive! It is an example of simplicity of heart at its best. Perhaps, like me, you have often longed for an increase of this ability to lay down the terrible burden of always needing to get your own way. Often you have prayed for its enlargement among the Christian fellowship. Doesn't our own failure make the Spirit-led experience of that pristine community all the more impressive? And the result is so uplifting: "And the word of God increased; and the number of the disciples multiplied greatly" (Acts 6:7).

This principle of giving way for the good of others is at the heart of Paul's ethical teaching. He counseled the believers at Corinth that, whenever there was a grievance among them, they should give in to each other rather than disgrace the name of Christ by taking the matter to a court of law. He queried, "Why not rather suffer wrong? Why not rather be defrauded?" (I Cor. 6:7). And why not? Christ suffered wrong for us and we are called to "follow in his steps. . . . When he was reviled, he did not revile in return; when he suffered, he did not threaten; but he trusted to him who judges justly" (I Pet. 2:21, 23).

Paul had earned the credentials to urge the Corinthians to surrender their own rights for the good of Christ and his Kingdom. He had done exactly the same among them. He had every right to receive financial support during the one and one-half years that he ministered among them. Pointedly he asked them, "Do we not have the right to our food and drink? . . . If we have sown spiritual good among you, is it too much if we reap your material benefits? If others share this rightful claim upon you, do not we still more?" Of course he did, and he knew it and they knew it. But he added, "Nevertheless, we have not made use of this right, but we endure anything rather than put an obstacle in the way of the Gospel of Christ" (I Cor. 9:4, 11–12). Rather than take advantage of his legitimate claim upon them, he provided for his needs through tent-making so that the word of Christ might abound in that city.

Having given these two examples, I hasten to warn that they can be easily twisted and turned into a new law that binds rather than liberates. I hope we will resist the temptation. There may well be times when going to court is the right and good thing to do, and often support for Gospel ministry should be freely given and graciously received. Paul was not giving a law but setting forth a perception into exactly how we can prefer one another in love (Rom. 12:10).

For Paul, the reason for acquiring money was not to build a nest egg but so he could share with others in need (Eph. 4:28). He urged the Corinthian believers to excel in giving to the Macedonian relief fund for the Christians at Jerusalem (II Cor. 8). James urged merchants to subordinate their buying and selling to the greater purposes of God. He wanted them to see that life was larger than business deals and accumulated wealth. He counseled perspective: "What is your life? For you are a mist that appears for a little time and then vanishes" (James 4:14).

Both Peter and Paul encouraged the practice of hospitality, which as any homemaker knows often involves considerable inconvenience for the sake of others (I Pet. 4:9, Rom. 12:13, I Tim. 3:2, I Tim. 1:8). James made it quite clear that if we discover brothers or sisters who are ill clad and lack daily food, we must give them what they need (James 2:14–17).

We are told in John's first Epistle that Christ laid down his life for us and that we ought to lay down our lives for the brethren. He then proceeded to describe in a concrete way how they were to lay down their lives for each other: "If anyone has the world's goods and sees his brother in need, yet closes his heart against him, how does God's love abide in him?" (I John 3:17). The question is obviously a rhetorical one. God's love is made flesh through these simple practical deeds in which we "by love serve one another" (Gal. 5:13, KJV).

Note how over and over the interest of others is the controlling principle. Banished is the obsession to demand one's own rights. Uppermost is the good of the fellowship and the advancement of Christ's Kingdom.

The Scandalous Invitation

Jesus Christ and all the writers of the New Testament call us to break free of mammon lust and live in joyous trust. Their radical criticism of wealth is combined with a spirit of unconditional generosity. They point to us a way of living in which everything we have we receive as a gift, and everything we have is cared for by God, and everything we have is available to others when it is right and good. This reality frames the heart of Christian simplicity. It is the means of liberation and power to do what is right and to overcome the forces of fear and avarice.

In our consideration of the Old Testament law of tithing, I promised to deal with the reason why none of the New Testament writers ever made the tithe the basis for Christian giving. That fact is quite conspicuous and quite startling, especially in the case of Paul. The relief fund for Jerusalem would have given him ample opportunity and reason to insist upon the tithe if he had wanted to make it normative for the Church. Why did Jesus, Paul, and all the Apostles refrain from making use of that well-established biblical tradition?

After having read through the New Testament witness to simplicity, and specifically its statements on wealth, the answer to that question is probably obvious to you. The tithe simply is not a sufficiently radical concept to embody the carefree unconcern for possessions that marks life in the Kingdom of God. Jesus Christ is the Lord of all our goods, not just ten percent. It is quite possible to obey the law of the tithe without ever dealing with our mammon lust. We can feel that our monthly check to the Church meets the new law of Jesus, and never once root out reigning covetousness and greed. It is quite possible to tithe and at the same time oppress the poor and needy. Jesus thundered against the Pharisees, "Woe to you, scribes and Pharisees, hypocrites! for you tithe mint and dill and cummin, and have neglected the weightier matters of the law, justice and mercy and faith; these you ought to have done, without neglecting the others" (Matt. 23:23). Mint, dill, and cummin were herbs of the kitchen garden, and hence any tithe on them would be infinitesimally small. How tragic to be meticulously trivial in the tithe and blind to justice and mercy and faith.

No doubt you noted that Jesus did not condemn the tithe as such: "These you ought to have done, without neglecting the others."* The tithe is not necessarily evil; it simply cannot provide a sufficient base for Jesus' call to carefree unconcern over provision. It fails to dethrone the rival god of materialism. It can never bring the freedom and liberality which is to characterize economic fellowship among the children of the Kingdom. Perhaps the tithe can be a beginning way to acknowledge God as the owner of all things, but it is only a beginning and not an ending.

When Jesus watched the voluntary offerings made in the temple treasury, he was moved by the sacrificial gift of the poor widow. What was it about her giving that touched him so? Jesus' comment on that simple act was, "For they all contributed out of their abundance; but she out of her poverty has put in everything she had, her whole living" (Mark 12:44).

Her giving had a certain reckless abandon to it. She evidenced an undivided devotion that fulfilled the command to

---

* Some scholars have felt that this phrase was a gloss, since it seems to spoil the point of the saying. There is, however, no manuscript evidence for this contention.

love God with all the heart, soul, mind, and strength. In fact, in Mark's Gospel this story follows closely on the heels of the two great commandments, as if to be a commentary upon them. A simple act, but one that crystallized the Christian witness. Here was a woman free from idolatry to mammon, devoid of greed and avarice. Here was a person in whom extravagant giving exceeded prudent thrift. Here was a widow, helpless and defenseless, who had learned to trust the Father in heaven for her needs day by day, one who sought first the Kingdom of God and his righteousness. Dare we follow her lead?

4. SIMPLICITY AMONG
THE SAINTS

I recommend to you holy simplicity.
　　　　　　　　　　　—Francis de Sales

History has a wonderful way of freeing us from the cult of the contemporary. It opens to us rich new vistas of "the communion of saints." We realize more pointedly than ever before that God has spoken in the past, and that we are not the only ones who have sought to live in faithful conformity to his word. It is humbling to be writing on Christian simplicity and to discover a fifteenth-century tome by Girolamo Savonarola entitled, *The Simplicity of the Christian Life*. Such experiences have a way of destroying all contemporary arrogance.

One remarkable feature of the devotional masters is the incredible sense of uniform witness in the midst of such diverse personalities. In the words of William James, "There is a certain composite photograph of saintliness."[1] People from different cultures and centuries exhibit a mutual verification that is well nigh amazing. And the necessity of Christian simplicity is one of their most consistent themes. People as divergent as Augustine of Hippo and Francis of Assisi, Blaise Pascal and Robert Barclay, Richard Baxter and John Wesley all called for simplicity of life.

We need to give attention to these voices rising out of the past, hear their witness, and follow their lead. We will investigate six different "models" of Christian simplicity. Obviously, they are only representative of the rich witness of Christians throughout the centuries.

There is no perfect model of anything. As long as we are

finite human beings we are bound to make mistakes and distort the truth. Movements throughout the history of the Church are no exception. Each group we will investigate evidenced deficiencies in one form or another. But this fact of human existence should in no way hinder our appreciation for their bright witness to a way of walking with God that is "free from outward cumbers."[2] In each case, particular attention will be given to the most prominent contribution to simplicity found in each movement. Finally, all of the concerns will be brought together by looking at three classical pieces of literature in the field of Christian simplicity.

Exuberant Caring and Sharing

In the period directly following the Apostolic Age there was an exuberant caring and sharing on the part of Christians that was unique in antiquity. Julian the apostate, an enemy of Christianity, admitted that "the godless Galileans fed not only their [poor] but ours also."[3] Tertullian wrote that the Christians' deeds of love were so noble that the pagan world confessed in astonishment, "See how they love one another."[4] Exactly what is it that these Christians did which elicited such a response from their enemies?

There was, first of all, an exceptional freedom to care for the needs of one another in the believing community. The *Didache* admonished Christians: "Thou shalt not turn away from him that is in want, but thou shalt share all things with thy brother, and shalt not say that they are thine own."[5] By A.D. 250 Christians in Rome were caring for some fifteen hundred needy people. In fact, their generosity was so profuse that Ignatius could say that they were "leading in love," and Bishop Dionysius of Corinth could note that they were sending "supplies to many churches in every city."[6] When Marcion, a well-to-do ship-owner from Asia Minor, joined with the Christians at Rome, he gave them the substantial sum of 200,000 sesterces.

We gain a helpful glimpse into the caring Christian community from I Clement, "Let everyone be subject to his neighbor. ... Let the rich man provide for the wants of the poor; and let the poor man bless God, because He hath given him one by whom his needs may be supplied."[7] Tertullian catalogued a long list of groups that were cared for by the Christian believers. They supported and buried the poor, supplied the needs of the boys and girls destitute of means, cared for the elderly that were confined to the house, provided for those who had suffered shipwreck, and gave to those who had been banished to islands or mines for their fidelity to Christ's cause.

Those who could work were encouraged to do so, in order that they might help those in need. The Pseudo-Clementine literature said that those who could work should do so, those who were unskilled should be helped to learn a skill, and those who could not work should be cared for by the fellowship.[8]

Christians also provided for those who lost their jobs because of their faith in Christ. It was assumed, for example, that an actor who became a Christian, and had to give up his profession because of its involvement in pagan mythology, would be cared for by the Church.

Christians were eager to help in other emergencies as well. When the Christians of Numidia were left homeless in A.D. 253 by invading nomads, Cyprian collected a spontaneous contribution for them of 100,000 sesterces from a small group in Carthage.

But their joyful sharing was not confined to Christians. These believers lived in such trustful simplicity toward God that they were liberated to share with any and all in need. Bishop John Chrysostom witnessed, "Every day the Church here feeds 3,000 people. Besides this, the church daily helps provide food and clothes for prisoners, the hospitalized, pilgrims, cripples, churchmen, and others."[9] When epidemics broke out in Carthage and Alexandria, Christians rushed to aid all in need. Justin Martyr said that the believing community gathered money in order to care for orphans, widows, the sick, those in prison, strangers, and "in a word takes care of all who are in need."[10]

These repeated and sustained sacrificial acts of charity cannot be explained in terms of ecclesiastical or secular politics. They grew out of a deep commitment to Christ and his call to care for the needy. These Christians genuinely believed that

God was the owner and giver of all good gifts. Their generosity was an imitation of God's generosity. They were free from anxiety because they knew that tomorrow was in God's hands. They lived in simplicity.

Perhaps no one has captured the exuberant spirit of simple caring and sharing better than the Christian philosopher Aristides, whose words (written in A.D. 125) are so moving that they are best quoted in full:

> They walk in all humility and kindness, and falsehood is not found among them, and they love one another. They despise not the widow, and grieve not the orphan. He that hath distributeth liberally to him that hath not. If they see a stranger, they bring him under their roof, and rejoice over him as if he were their own brother: for they call themselves brethren, not after the flesh, but after the Spirit of God; but when one of their poor passes away from the world, and any of them see him, then he provides for his burial according to his ability; and if they hear that any of their number is imprisoned or oppressed for the name of their Messiah, all of them provide for his needs, and if it is possible that he may be delivered, they deliver him. And if there is among them a man that is poor and needy, and they have not an abundance of necessaries, they fast two or three days that they may supply the needy with their necessary food.[11]

This model of simplicity speaks to our condition. How desperately we need today to discover new creative ways of caring and sharing with any in need.

The Power of Renunciation

The power of renunciation as seen in the Desert Fathers is a second model of Christian simplicity.

As the persecution of the early Christians began to die out, it was no longer possible to witness for Christ by martyrdom. But the world had not changed its antipathy to the Gospel message, only its tactics. Persecution was replaced by assimilation.

For the Desert Fathers, the flight to the desert was a way of escaping conformity to the world. The world, including the Church, had become so dominated by secular materialism that, for them, the only way to witness against it was to withdraw from it. Thomas Merton writes in the introduction to his *Wisdom of the Desert*, "Society . . . was regarded by the Desert Fathers as a shipwreck from which each single individual man had to swim for his life."[12]

They were seeking to revive true Christian devotion and simplicity of life by intense renunciation. Their experience has particular relevance, because modern society is uncomfortably like the world that they attacked so vigorously. Their world asked, "How can I get more?" The Desert Fathers asked, "What can I do without?" Their world asked, "How can I find myself?" The Desert Fathers asked, "How can I lose myself?" Their world asked, "How can I win friends and influence people?" The Desert Fathers asked, "How can I love God?"

Anthony, the "father of monks" (A.D. 251–356), was about eighteen years old when he heard the Gospel words, "Go, sell what you possess and give to the poor . . . and come, follow me" (Matt. 19:21). Going out from the church, he immediately gave away his inherited land, sold all of his possessions, and distributed the proceeds among the poor, saving only enough to care for his sister. After living at the edge of his village for a time, he retreated into the desert, where for twenty years he lived in complete solitude. In the solitude he was forced to face his false, empty self. He learned to die to the opinions of others. He came out of a bondage to human beings. Violent and many were the temptations he faced.

When he emerged from the solitude of the desert, he was marked with graciousness, love, kindness, endurance, meekness, freedom from anger, and the practice of prayer. People recognized in him a unique compassion and power. Many sought him out for spiritual counsel and healing prayer. Even the Emperor Constantine sought his advice. For many years he had an effective and varied ministry. In the final years of his life he retreated again to the solitude of the desert, where he died in his 105th year.

The Desert Fathers renounced things in order to know what it meant to have the single eye of simplicity toward God. They were the *Athletae Dei*, the athletes of God, who sought to strip away all hindrances. There is no question that there were excesses in the monasticism of the Desert Fathers, but no more so than the excesses evidenced in the Church of today in the opposite direction.

The renunciation of the Desert Fathers had great transforming power. They renounced possessions in order to learn detachment. These men and women of the desert gained a great freedom when they surrendered the need to possess. Among the sayings of the Fathers is the story of an important dignitary who gave a basket of gold pieces to a priest in the desert, asking him to disperse it among the brethren. "They have no need of it," replied the priest. The wealthy benefactor insisted and set the basket of coins at the doorway of the Church, asking the priest to tell the brethren, "Whoso hath need, let him take it." No one touched it, or even cared enough to look at it. Edified, and no doubt astonished, the man left with his basket of gold.[13]

Detachment frees us from the control of others. No longer can we be manipulated by people who hold our livelihoods in their hands. Things do not entice our imaginations, people do not dominate our destinies.

The Desert Fathers renounced speech in order to learn compassion. A charming story is told of Abbot Macarius, who said to the brethren in the Church in Scete, "Brethren, flee." Perplexed, one of the brothers asked, "How can we fly further than this, seeing we are here in the desert?" Macarius placed his finger to his mouth and said, "Flee from this." When Arsenius, the Roman educator who gave up his status and wealth for the solitude of the desert, prayed, "Lord, lead me into the way of salvation," he heard a voice saying, "Be silent."[14]

Silence frees us from the need to control others. One reason we can hardly bear to remain silent is that it makes us feel so helpless. We are accustomed to relying upon words to manage and control others. A frantic stream of words flows from us in an attempt to straighten others out. We want so desperately for them to agree with us, to see things our way. We evaluate people, judge people, condemn people. We devour people with our words. Silence is one of the deepest Disciplines of the Spirit simply because it puts the stopper on that.

When we become quiet enough to let go of people, we learn compassion for them. We can be with people in their hurt and need. We can speak a word out of our inner silence that will set them free. Anthony knew that the true test of spirituality was in the freedom to live among people compassionately: "With our neighbor there is life and death: for if we do good to our brother, we shall do good to God: but if we scandalize our brother, we sin against Christ."[15]

The Desert Fathers renounced activity in order to learn prayer. Prayer was at the heart of the desert experience. These athletes of God sought to strip away all superfluous things, so they could concentrate on the one thing most needful. Prayer was the great work of their lives. Abbot Agatho declared, "There is no labor so great as praying to God. . . . With any other labor that a man undertakes in the life of religion, however instant and close he keeps to it, he hath some rest: but prayer hath the travail of a mighty conflict to one's last breath."[16]

Prayer frees us to be controlled by God. To pray is to change. There is no greater liberating force in the Christian life than prayer. To enter the gaze of the Holy is never to be the same. To bathe in the Light in quiet wonder and glad surrender is to be slowly, permanently transformed. There is a richer inward orientation, a deeper hunger for communion. We feel as if we are being taken over by a new control Center, and so we are.

Few if any of us will be led to the forms of renunciation that characterize the Desert Fathers. But all of us need to seek God for "wineskins" that will build into our lives the simplicity of detachment, compassion, and prayer.

The Joy of Simplicity

The poor little monk of Assisi, St. Francis, and his jubilant band comprise yet another model of Christian simplicity. They tramped the earth inebriated with the love of God, and filled with ecstasy. Buoyant joy was the hallmark of their simplicity. Francis (A.D. 1182–1226) is one of the most winsome figures in the history of the Christian faith. Born in the ancient Italian town of Assisi of wealthy parents, his adolescent years were spent as a charming and carefree playboy. A leader among the local young aristocracy, he often initiated their fun-loving revelries.

Illness and a military disappointment were among the influences that began to lead the sensitive Francis through a lengthy series of intense struggles of the spirit. The climax came in 1206 when his enraged father brought him before the bishop, to disinherit him. Francis stripped himself naked and walked away determined to follow the Lord's bidding into apostolic poverty.

Moved by his joyousness under oppression and his espousal of Lady Poverty, many flocked to the young Francis. Three years after the decisive call had come to Francis, a young girl of sixteen, Clara, sought to join the movement. Thus a woman's branch of the Franciscans, the Poor Ladies or Poor Clares, came into being. In time, this jubilant group of men and women became one of the largest and most influential orders in the Catholic faith.

The early Franciscan movement had an unusual combination of mystical contemplation and evangelistic fervor. Paul Sabatier, perhaps the most authoritative biographer of St. Francis, wrote of Francis' missionary zeal, "Perfectly happy, he felt himself more and more impelled to bring others to share his happiness and to proclaim in the four corners of the world how he had attained it."[17] Enthusiastically, he traversed much of Italy, preached to the Sultan in Egypt, and sought to engage in ministry among the Moslems in Spain. He was a captivating speaker, and his deep conviction and radiant love aroused an almost delirious enthusiasm on the part of the people.[18]

He sent out his Brothers Minor—Little Brothers—all over Europe and to Morocco. He referred to his humble band as "God's jugglers," whose task was to "revive the hearts of men and lead them into spiritual joy."[19]

The Friars Minor not only preached, but also sang. Exuberant and joyful, they were often caught up in ecstasy as they worshiped. With the soul of a poet, Francis would improvise their hymns. Best known is his *Canticle of the Sun,* with its celebration of Brother Sun and Sister Moon, Brother Wind and Sister Water. It is a joyous adoration of God as the Creator of all good things.

A love for the creation certainly marked these simple Friars. They lived close to the earth and took special joy in it. On one occasion Francis and Brother Masseo went begging bread in a small village. Returning with a few dried crusts, they searched until they found a spring for drinking and a flat rock for a table. As they ate their meager lunch Francis exclaimed several times, "Oh Brother Masseo, we do not deserve such a great treasure as this!" Finally, Brother Masseo protested that such poverty could hardly be called a treasure. They had no cloth, no knife, no dish, no bowl, no house, no table. Elated, Francis replied, "That is what I consider a great treasure—where nothing has been prepared by human labor. But everything here has been supplied by Divine Providence, as is evidenced in the baked bread, fine stone table, and the clear spring." Joyfully they finished their meal and then journeyed on toward France "rejoicing and praising the Lord in song."[20]

A joyous trust characterized their simplicity. At one time Francis gathered some five thousand Friars in an open plain for something akin to a camp meeting among the Brothers. Saint Dominic and several other prominent people had come to watch the event. At one point Francis rose and delivered a moving sermon concluding with the command that the Friars not have "any care or anxiety concerning anything to eat or drink or the other things necessary for the body, but to concentrate only on praying and praising God. And leave all your worries about your body to Christ, because He takes special care of you."

Hearing this, Dominic was distressed at the seemingly imprudent order. However, within a short period of time people from all the surrounding towns began arriving, bringing with them generous supplies of food. A great celebrative feast followed as the monks rejoiced in this provision of God. Dominic was so moved by the scene that he meekly knelt before Francis and said, "God is truly taking care of these holy little poor men, and I did not realize it. Therefore I promise henceforth to observe the holy poverty of the Gospel."[21]

Francis knew joy, but it was the joy rooted in the Cross, not in escape from it. The delightful story is told about how Francis taught Brother Leo the meaning of perfect joy. As the two walked together in the rain and bitter cold, Francis reminded Leo of all the things that people believed would bring joy, adding each time, "Perfect joy is not in that." Finally, in exasperation Brother Leo asked, "I beg you in God's name to tell me where perfect joy is." Whereupon, Francis began enumerating the most humiliating, self-abasing things he could imagine, adding each time, "Oh, Brother Leo, write that perfect joy is there." To explain and conclude the matter he told him, "Above all the graces and gifts of the Holy Spirit which Christ gives to His friends is that of conquering oneself and willingly enduring sufferings, insults, humiliations, and hardships for the love of Christ."[22]

The life of St. Francis gives us a healthy model of celibacy. (Examples of unhealthy celibacy abound in the history of the Church.) This matter of the single life should not be taken lightly. To be quite blunt about it, celibacy is necessary for some forms of simplicity. Francis could not have done what he did if he had not been single. Nor could Jesus.

Celibacy is not essential to simplicity, but it is essential to some expressions of simplicity. If we want to live like Francis, we had better not be married. If we want to be married, we had better not try to live like Francis. The failure to understand this simple fact has caused a great deal of misery in human society.

Francis and his Friars Minor knew the joy of the Lord. They were stamped by simple love and joyous trust. They led a cheerful, happy revolt against the spirit of materialism and double-mindedness. Nothing is more needed today than a simplicity distinguished by triumphant joy.

Theology in the Cause of Simplicity

The Protestant Reformation provides a crucial insight into the theological foundation for simplicity. Luther saw that the encrusted traditions of the Middle Ages undermined the authority of Scripture, and so lifted high the principle of *sola scriptura*, Scripture alone. He sought to cut down the complex system of merit that had arisen in the Roman Catholic Church with the Scriptural principle of *sola gratia,* grace alone. He endeavored to provide a basis for faithful living that stood over against the works righteousness of his day, by insisting on the biblical principle of *sola fide,* faith alone. The result was a simplification in both doctrine and life.

Martin Luther dealt with the matter of simplicity in the most profoundly practical way in his book *The Freedom of a Christian.* What he saw in such sharp focus was that the liberty of the Gospel sets us free to serve our neighbor with singleness of purpose. If our salvation is by grace alone we no longer need to keep juggling a myriad of religious duties to get right with God. We are free from constantly taking our own spiritual temperature.

Our freedom from sin allows us to serve others. Before, all our serving was for our benefit, a means to somehow get right with God. Only because the grace of God has been showered upon us are we enabled to give that same grace to others. Luther expresses this thesis in his famous paradox: "A Christian is a perfectly free lord of all, subject to none. A Christian is a perfectly dutiful servant of all, subject to all."[23] Through the grace of God alone, and not by any work of righteousness on our part, we come into the glorious liberty of the Gospel. We are all lords and kings and priests, as Luther put it. We are set free from the law of sin and death.

But this freedom is not for our sake alone—it is also a freedom to serve others. Until we are righteous we cannot really do righteous deeds no matter how hard we try. Luther said, "Good works do not make a good man, but a good man does good works; evil works do not make a wicked man, but a wicked man does evil works."[24]

Let's illustrate this matter in a simple way. A poor artist may paint many pictures, but he will not paint any good pictures. An inferior contractor may build many homes, but he will not construct any good homes. The person who is still bound to sin and enslaved to others is not free to truly love his neighbor.

A moment's reflection on our part confirms the truth of Luther's insight. If we are still in bondage to sin, our serving will flow out of that center. We will not have the single eye that gives light to all we do. Pride and fear and manipulation will control our actions. We will not be free to serve our neighbor in simplicity. If we are still in bondage to others, our serving will flow out of that center. We will be controlled by a desire to impress them, or receive their help. Without Gospel liberty, we will forever measure who we are by the yardstick of others. We will not be free to serve our neighbor in simplicity.

But once the grace of God has broken into our lives, we are free. When we are free from the control of our neighbor, we are able to obey God. And as we obey God with a single heart, we are given a new power and desire to serve our neighbor, from whom we are now free. We have become "servants of our neighbors, and yet lords of all."[25] We know simplicity of life. Luther concludes, "A Christian lives not in himself, but in Christ and his neighbor. Otherwise he is not a Christian."[26]

John Calvin developed a theology of the state that was the source of tremendous social power. While Luther tended to separate the Church from the state, Calvin tried to integrate them, and to produce a just social order by giving the controlling power to the righteous. He viewed Christians as the instruments of God in the transformation of the entire society.

This approach took seriously the role of Christian political activism. Christians must concern themselves with matters of justice and service. A social order that caters to the privileged elite, while masses of its people are deprived of necessities, cannot be tolerated. Christians have a responsibility to bring social justice into realization. These are concerns close to the heart of Christian simplicity. Concerning government authorities, Calvin could say, "They are not to rule for their own interest, but for the public good; nor are they endued with unbridled power, but what is restricted to the wellbeing of their subjects."[27] In other words, the state has a God-given task to provide justice for all people alike, and Christians have a responsibility to see that it fulfills this function.

Christians are to commend the state when it does justice, and condemn it when it fails to bring justice. More than that, Christians are to actively involve themselves in the state to work for the cause of justice. However much we may debate the specific means Calvin himself used to realize this conviction, we must join him in the conviction.

Luther and Calvin help us to understand the importance of

both liberty and justice in our search for Christian simplicity. We need to join with Luther in seeking the freedom of the Gospel which allows us to serve our neighbor in love. We need to join with Calvin in seeking social justice in all of society, which allows human beings to live in peace.

Hearing and Obeying

Holy obedience to the living voice of Christ brought birth to a vigorous form of simplicity among seventeenth-century Quakers. Offense at the gluttonous excess of his day led young George Fox (A.D. 1624–1691) to seek after God, a seeking that reached an important turning point when he heard a voice which said, "There is one, even Christ Jesus, that can speak to thy condition."[28] And so from the very outset Quakerism centered in the conviction that the voice of Christ could be heard and his will obeyed. This listening to Jesus Christ is what led the early Quakers to a radical simplicity testimony.

If the early Quaker preaching were to be brought into one sentence, it would be, "Christ has come to teach his people himself." These people were convinced that Christ was the fulfillment of the "prophet like unto Moses" who had been prophesied (Deut. 18:15–18, KJV). As prophet, Christ is able to teach us the righteousness of God. We can hear his voice if we will listen. His teaching will always be consistent with the Scriptures, since the Scriptures give us a faithful record of Christ's teaching to the Apostles and Prophets.

Not only does Christ our Prophet teach us, but he gives us the power to obey. George Fox declares that "God doth draw people from their unrighteousness and unholiness to Christ the righteous and holy one, the great prophet whom Moses said God would raise up whom people should hear in all things," and he urges all Christians to consider "whether you do believe that God raised up this prophet Christ Jesus? And if so, whether you do hear him?"[29]

A simplicity that took exception to many of the customs of the day resulted from this hearing and obeying the word of Christ. The early Quakers witnessed to simplicity in their attire: they rejected the gaudy superficial fashions that abounded in that day, and instead adopted the plain clothing of the working class. They refused to remove their hats in deference to the nobility, because they were convinced that all people deserved equal honor.

They witnessed to simplicity in their speech, in which honesty and integrity were the distinguishing characteristics. It was said that a Quaker's word was as good as his bond. "Thee" and "thou," which at the time were used for everyone but the elite, they used when speaking to peasant and king alike. They refused to take oaths because it implied a double standard of truth. They needed no oath to guarantee that they spoke the truth—their Yes was Yes, and their No was No.

They witnessed to simplicity by vigorously opposing injustice and oppression. They condemned the "price fixing" of the day, which discriminated against the poor and needy, and insisted instead on a one-price system for all. Their writings were shot through with outraged cries against the conspicuous consumption of the wealthy because of its connection with the poverty that was rampant in the land. In *No Cross, No Crown*, William Penn scathingly denounced the practice of 95 percent of agriculture going to feed "the inordinate lusts and delicious appetites" of 5 percent of the population.[30] When the wealthy rationalized their extravagance under the excuse that it provided employment for the poor, George Fox rebutted, "If you say how shall the poor live if you do not wear that; give them all that money which you bestow upon all that gorgeous attire, and needless things, to nourish them, that they may live without making vanities."[31]

These early "Publishers of Truth," as they called themselves, took with utter seriousness the task of hearing the voice of Christ and obeying his word. They would ask, "What does it mean to live faithful lives in our day?" and they fully expected to receive an answer. Christ spoke to them through the Scripture, he also moved directly upon the heart of the attentive listener, and he spoke most powerfully when they were gathered together in worship. The corporate commitment to listen to Christ produced corporate convictions, for their Teacher promised to create unity among them (Matt. 18:18–20).

But to hear Christ's word was not enough. They also waited

to receive the power to obey that word. And it was the conviction that they would actually receive the power to obey the instruction given them which gave early Friends such vitality. They walked cheerfully upon the earth in the power of the Lord. They called their struggle "the Lamb's War," and fully believed the Lamb of God would give them victory over all "vanity, customs, and fashions of this generation."[32] In every detail they sought to live in holy obedience.

We who live in a world of half-truths and rationalizations and intellectual gymnastics that keep us from hearing and obeying the word of Christ need to hear their witness. Because we live in a different culture, we must once again ask what it means to live faithful lives in our day. But we must ask fully expecting to receive an answer and fully expecting to be given the power to obey the call.

Simplicity in Action

Examples abound of Christian simplicity in the task of evangelism, in the service of the poor, and in the cause of social justice. The vigorous evangelistic efforts of John Wesley and the early Methodists are well known. The simplicity of their lifestyle gave integrity to the Gospel they preached. Wesley is reported to have told his sister, "Money never stays with me. It would burn me if it did. I throw it out of my hands as soon as possible, lest it should find its way within my heart." He told everyone that, if at his death he had more than ten pounds (about $23) in his possession, people had the privilege of calling him a robber.[33] Near the end of his life he wrote in his journal very simply, "I left no money to anyone in my will, because I had none."[34]

Francis Asbury, the "Apostle of American Methodism," remained single all of his life and lived on a very meager income in order to devote all his energies to the advancement of Christ's cause in America. His single-hearted devotion is evidenced from a notation in his journal as he sailed to the Colonies, "Whither am I going? To the new world. What to do? To gain honor? No, if I know my own heart. To get money? No. I am going to live to God and to bring others so to do."[35] Such simplicity of life in the task of evangelism could be multiplied a thousand fold among the faithful army of itinerant Methodist preachers.

No one can read the Journal of David Brainerd without being struck by the utter simplicity of his life, and his single-minded devotion to bring Christ to the American Indian. Obsessive status seeking and compulsive extravagance were antithetical to his life and message.

From its inception, the modern missionary movement was rooted in sacrifice and simplicity. From William Cary to Adoniram Judson, from J. Hudson Taylor to C. T. Studd, they leave us a legacy of commitment to simplicity. As Hudson Taylor prepared to bring the Gospel to the great throngs of inland China, he taught himself to endure hardness and to economize in order to help people in need. He said, "I soon found that I could live upon very much less than I had previously thought possible. Butter, milk and other luxuries I ceased to use, and found that by living mainly on oatmeal and rice, with occasional variations, a very small sum was sufficient for my needs." In this way he was able to use two-thirds of his income for other purposes. He wrote, "My experience was that the less I spent on myself and the more I gave to others, the fuller of happiness and blessing did my soul become."[36]

In our own century, consider the example of Sadhu Sundar Singh, the man who has done more than any other to incarnate the Christian faith into the life and culture of India. Adopting the saffron robe of the Indian Sadhus, or holy men, Sundar Singh lived a life of extreme simplicity as he tramped the length and breadth of India. His bearded figure, radiant smile, and compelling preaching became widely known in many countries. He disappeared in 1929 while on an evangelistic mission into Tibet, presumably martyred for his faith in Christ.

Christians have also raised the standard of simplicity in the service of the poor. At the early age of twenty, Antoine Frédéric Ozanam persuaded some of his fellow students to help him in serving the destitute and underprivileged of France. It was the beginning of the St. Vincent de Paul Society. Begun in 1833, it quickly spread to many countries.

William Booth established the Salvation Army out of a

burning desire to help the dregs of the industrial urban civilization. Ministering among the worst slums of London, Booth first
sought to bring these broken and dispossessed people into the
churches. Unwilling to receive them, the churches rejected
Booth and his followers. Booth turned to unconventional open-
air meetings on the streets, complete with drums, tambourines,
and trumpets. His book, *In Darkest England and the Way
Out,* is a scathing exposé of the economic, social, and moral
conditions in the slums, and in it Booth made daring proposals
to overcome these conditions. Along with other things he called
for a poor man's bank, rescue homes for prostitutes, and model
suburban villages.[37]

Robert Raikes established the Sunday School movement in
an attempt to provide educational opportunities for the extremely poor on the only day they did not have to work—Sunday. George Müller has inspired many to faithful ministry by
his homes for the orphans of Bristol, which were begun and
maintained entirely through prayer for their material means.
George Williams founded the Young Men's Christian Association (YMCA) to provide evangelistic, social, and athletic opportunities for the lower income levels of the white collar class.

In the twentieth century, one thinks immediately of Albert
Schweitzer. Extremely versatile, Schweitzer was a New Testament scholar, a distinguished organist and authority on Bach,
and an accomplished philosopher and theologian. He chose,
however, to give the bulk of his adult career to serving the people of French Equatorial Africa as a medical missionary.

Simplicity also has been a vigorous force in the cause of social justice. David Livingstone is well known for missionary ex-
ploits and especially for his determined efforts to abolish what
he called "the open sore of the world," the African slave trade.
Living in great simplicity, both in inward spirit and in outward
lifestyle, he persistently pleaded the cause of the helpless of
Africa. The horrors of the slave trade, said Livingstone, were
beyond exaggeration. "To overdraw its evils is a simple impossibility."[38] Among the last words which he was to write in his
journal were these: "I will forget all my cold, hunger, suffering
and trials, if I can be the means of putting a stop to this cursed
traffic."[39]

Clarence Jordan has made an important imprint upon twentieth-century America by his courageous life of simplicity in the cause of social justice. The founder of Koinonia Farm and author of the Cotton Patch version of the New Testament, he has sometimes been called a theologian in overalls. He withstood harassment, economic boycott, and gunfire from nightriders in order to make a bold social witness for peace, community, and racial equality.

Jordan began his experiment in racial reconciliation in 1942 on a farm near Americus, Georgia, and he remained there until his death in 1969. In everything he was marked by simplicity of spirit and life. His call for justice and peace and simplicity in the context of authentic Christian community is a challenge to our perennial culture-conforming tendencies.[40]

And today many groups have arisen which have battled for justice out of Christian conviction. Among some of the better known of these groups are the Berkeley Christian Coalition in Berkeley, California, which publishes *Radix;* Voice of Calvary in Mendenhall, Mississippi, which publishes *The Quiet Revolution;* Jubilee Fellowship in Philadelphia, Pennsylvania, which publishes *The Other Side;* the Catholic Worker Movement in many American urban centers, which publishes *The Catholic Worker;* and The People's Christian Coalition in Washington, D. C., which publishes *Sojourners.* Whatever may be the shortcomings of these many movements, certainly one of their greatest assets has been their understanding of how intrinsic Christian simplicity is in the cause of justice.

Words to Live By

No investigation into simplicity in the history of the Church is complete without at least a brief perusal of its literature. We possess a rich heritage of writings on this topic from Clement's *The Rich Man's Salvation* and Cyprian's *On Good Works and Alms Giving,* to the *Letters of St. Jerome* and the works of Eckhard, Tauler, and Suso; from the writings of the Radical Reformation to the *Epistles of George Fox* and William Penn's *No Cross, No Crown.* And, of course, many modern writers have addressed this subject with new vigor, including Francis

Florand in *Stages of Simplicity*, Arthur Gish in *Beyond the Rat Race*, and Ronald Sider in *Rich Christians in An Age of Hunger*.

I have chosen to look at three representative writings which, taken together, give us a composite picture of the concern for Christian simplicity in the history of the church: *The Simplicity of the Christian Life*, by Girolamo Savonarola; *Purity of Heart Is to Will One Thing*, by Søren Kierkegaard; and *The Journal* and *A Plea for the Poor* by John Woolman.

Girolamo Savonarola's *The Simplicity of the Christian Life* is actually a discussion of the nature of the good life. He is seeking to answer the question, "What makes people happy?" Of all created beings, writes Savonarola, only humans have to struggle to discover their proper role in the whole scheme of things. We are the only ones who seek for meaning, purpose, happiness. The blessed life, says Savonarola, is not found primarily in sensual pursuits nor in intellectual pursuits nor even in spiritual pursuits, as normally understood. No, the happy life is rooted in the grace of God and discovered in imitating the life and teachings of Jesus. The main means through which this simple life of the *Imitatio Christi* occurs are prayer and love.

Having laid the foundation, Savonarola proceeds with two crucial chapters: "Simplicity of the Heart" and "Exterior Simplicity." "Each Christian," declared Savonarola, "ought to try to come to perfect simplicity" of the heart.[41] Even the natural order witnesses to the fact that the more inwardly simple or unified something is the more perfect it is. In the spiritual realm, this inner heart simplicity is discovered in having the crucified Christ as the unifying force of all our affections and aspirations.

Exterior simplicity flows from this true interior simplicity. We can see this in the creation, says Savonarola. A tree or flower is pleasing to the eye because it reflects an inner harmony and unity. The same is true of our lives. If we enter into the simplicity of God we will have an exterior quality of life marked by unity and peace. "The true Christian greatly loves and adores exterior simplicity," comments Savonarola. In even stronger language, he goes on to add, "He who does not love exterior simplicity is not able to live the Christian life."[42]

But we must remember, counseled Savonarola, that simplicity in exterior things does not come to all equally. Some occupations demand a greater use of material goods. Also, there needs to be a certain ordinary common sense (he uses the word "prudence") employed in deciding what we should do without. In fact, Savonarola adds, it is not wrong to seek those things necessary for a "decent state," and if we have simplicity of heart we can distinguish between those things that are necessary for a decent state and those things that are superfluous. The best guides in these decisions, says Savonarola, are the Sacred Scriptures and spiritual discernment. He then concludes with a chapter on the danger of wealth, and a chapter on the happiness of the Christian life.

Kierkegaard's *Purity of Heart Is to Will One Thing* stands as a vigorous statement of inward simplicity. While Descartes said, "I think, therefore I am," Kierkegaard said in effect, "I am, therefore I must decide." Slowly, carefully he strips away all of our rationalizations and barriers to willing one thing until we stand as a single individual at the crossroads. Significantly, the book itself is dedicated to "that solitary individual," and relentlessly it forces us to come, naked and alone, before God, where we must decide how to live. In reality, the book is an extended commentary on words of the Apostle James, "Draw near to God and he will draw near to you. Cleanse your hands, you sinners, and purify your hearts, you men of double mind" (James 4:8).

Some have misunderstood the message of *Purity of Heart* by assuming that it is possible to will one thing, and that unspeakably evil, as in Adolf Hitler. On the contrary, says Kierkegaard, "the person who wills one thing that is not the Good . . . does not truly will one thing. It is a delusion, an illusion, a deception, a self-deception that he wills only one thing. For in his innermost being he is, he is bound to be, double-minded."[43] His point is a simple one. God is the only whole, satisfying, unifying reality in the universe. Only God is one, and he alone encompasses the good. To desire anything outside of God is not to will *one* thing but "a multiple of things, a dispersion, the toy of changeableness, and the prey of corruption!" No desire can be fully satisfied when it is outside of God, and the individual becomes "not merely double-minded but thousand-minded, and at variance with himself."[44]

Purity of heart, then, is found in willing only the good, which is God. To do so unifies and simplifies everything. But Kierkegaard warns that to desire the good for the sake of the reward is not to will one thing, to desire the good out of fear of punishment is not to will one thing, to desire the good out of self-centered willfulness is not to will one thing, to desire the good with a half-hearted commitment is not to will one thing. Utter abandonment, absolute commitment to the good, to God, is the requirement for willing one thing, for purity of heart.

Kierkegaard has pressed home for us how essential inner simplicity is to our task. Even when we are seeking God, but doing so out of a duplicitous motivation, though our words and deeds may seem virtuous we will be double-minded at best. No, Kierkegaard makes it clear; our inward disposition must be centered, focused, synoptic if we want to know that purity of heart that is Christian simplicity.

The Journal of John Woolman has stood the test of time and is now universally recognized as one of our great devotional classics. Often published with *The Journal* is *A Plea for the Poor*. Together they stand as a witness to the necessity of both inward and outward simplicity, the one flowing from the other. It would be hard to imagine a more eloquent testimony to the grace of Christian simplicity.

Woolman first dealt with the issue of simplicity on a personal level. A businessman in retail goods, a tailor, and a nurseryman, he soon found that his trade "increased every year, and the way to large business appeared open, but I felt a stop in my mind." The hesitancy he felt was not due to a fear of entering into too affluent a lifestyle. That matter had been settled long ago as he witnessed, "I had, in a good degree, learned to be content with a plain way of living."

The real problem was two-fold. First, there was the issue of compromise found in marketing items that catered to people's vanity more than they served real needs. He writes, "Things that served chiefly to please the vain mind in people, I was not easy to trade in; seldom did it; and whenever I did I found it weakened me as a Christian."[45] The second and deciding issue was the need to be free from "cumbers" in order to give unin-hibited attention to the Lord's call upon him. Finally, he felt he must cut back his business. This set him free to engage in a remarkable traveling ministry that was to be a major force in causing Quakers to rid themselves of slavery before America had gained independence from the British Empire.

Passage after passage is filled with tender references to the plight of slaves and slave-owners alike. He saw with unusual clarity the connection between covetousness and slavery.

The Lord . . . is graciously moving in the hearts of people to draw them off from the desire of wealth and to bring them into such a humble, lowly way of living that they may see their way clearly to repair to the standard of true righteousness, and may not only break the yoke of oppres-sion, but may know him to be their strength and support in times of outward affliction.[46]

His *Plea for the Poor* is a tract for our times. In it, Woolman addresses affluent America and asks us to tender our hearts to the needs of the poor. It is filled with practical suggestions on how we can identify with the poor and needy of the earth, espe-cially those who "labor for us out of our sight."[47] He even rec-ommends that we take up the work of the poor for a time in order to *feel* their burdens.

In a small way, we have entered the "communion of saints" in this chapter. We have heard the witness of men and women throughout the centuries who have sought to walk with God faithfully and simply. Their message is clear, and is perhaps best summed up in the words of Francis de Sales, "In every-thing, love simplicity."[48]

PART II

The Practice

5. INWARD SIMPLICITY: THE DIVINE CENTER

Oh, blessed simplicity, that seizes swiftly what cleverness, tired out in the service of vanity, may grasp but slowly.
—*Søren Kierkegaard*

In his lofty mythology, *The Silmarillion,* J. R. R. Tolkien gives a penetrating picture into the effects of inward simplicity, "But the delight and pride of Aüle is in the deed of making, and in the thing made, and neither in possession nor in his own mastery; wherefore he gives and hoards not, and is free from care, passing ever on to some new work."[1] What an inviting picture of movement and work in harmony with the divine Center of the universe. And what a contrast to the frantic and often frustrated rush of our daily lives.

We dash here and there desperately trying to fulfill the many obligations that press in upon us. We jerk back and forth between business commitments and family responsibilities. While we are busy responding to the needs of child or spouse, we feel guilty about neglecting the demands of work. When we respond to the pressures of work, we fear we are failing our family. In those rare times when we are able to juggle the two successfully, the wider issues of nation and world whisper pestering calls to service. If anyone needs a simplification of life, we do.

What will set us free from this bondage to the ever spiraling demands that are placed upon us? The answer is found in the grace of Christian simplicity. This virtue, once worked into our lives, will unify the demands of our life. It will prune and trim gently and in the right places. It brings a liberty of soul that eliminates constant reversions to ourselves.

Life at the Center

I still remember the rainy February morning inside a Washington, D.C., airport many years ago. Exhausted, I slumped into a chair to wait for my flight. As always, I had brought reading material in order to make good use of free moments. For the first time in my life I opened Thomas Kelly's *Testament of Devotion.*

Immediately, he caught my attention by describing perfectly my condition and the condition of so many I knew: "We feel honestly the pull of many obligations and try to fulfill them all. And we are unhappy, uneasy, strained, oppressed, and fearful we shall be shallow."[2] Yes, I had to confess I was in those words. To all who saw me I was confident and in command, but inwardly I was tired and scattered. Then my eyes came upon words of hope and promise, "We have hints that there is a way of life vastly richer and deeper than all this hurried existence, a life of unhurried serenity and peace and power. If only we could slip over into that Center!"[3] Instinctively, I knew that he was speaking of a reality beyond what I had known. Please understand me, I was not ungodly and irreverent, just the opposite. My problem was that I was so serious, so concerned to do what was right, that I felt compelled to respond to every call to service. And, after all, they were wonderful opportunities to minister in Christ's name.

Then came the sentence that was to prompt an inner revolution: "We have seen and known some people who seem to have found this deep Center of living, where the fretful calls of life are integrated, where No as well as Yes can be said with confidence."[4] This ability to say Yes and No out of the divine Center was foreign to me. I had always prayed over decisions, and yet I too often responded on the basis of whether or not the action would put me in a favorable light. To say Yes to pleas for help or opportunities to serve usually carried an aura of spirituality and sacrifice. I could say Yes easily, but I did not have the ability to say No. What would people think of me if I refused?

Alone, I sat in the airport watching the rain splatter against the window. Tears fell on my coat. It was a holy place, an altar, the chair where I sat. I was never to be the same. Quietly, I asked God to give me the ability to say No when it was right and good.

Back home, I was once again caught up into a flurry of activity. But I had made one decision—Friday nights were to be reserved for the family. It was a small decision at the time; nobody but I really knew about it. I had told the family in a casual, off-hand fashion; they did not know it was a covenant commitment, a crossroads decision. Nor did I, really. It just seemed the right thing to do, hardly what one would call a God-given directive.

But then the phone call came. It was a denominational executive. Would I be willing to speak to this group on Friday night? There it was, another wonderful opportunity. My response was casual, almost unconscious, "Oh, no, I can't." The reply was also casual, "Oh, do you have another commitment?" I felt trapped. (In those days I did not know that I could quite legitimately say that I did indeed have a very important commitment.) Cautiously but purposefully, I answered simply, "No," with no attempt to justify or explain my decision. There followed a long period of silence which seemed to last an eternity. I could amost feel the words, "Where is your dedication?" traveling through the telephone wires. I knew I had made a decision that made me seem less spiritual to one for whom I genuinely cared. After a moment we shared a few pleasantries and then hung up; but as the phone hit the receiver, inwardly I shouted, "Hallelujah." I had yielded to the Center. I had touched the margin of simplicity, and the effect was electrifying.

The incident was so small and insignificant that it is almost embarrassing to relate it to you. I'm sure my denominational friend does not even recall the phone conversation. And yet somehow I had turned a corner. Even now I sometimes wish I could say that something terribly important precipitated the change. But there it was, a trivial event, yet it had changed everything. Perhaps it has been that way for you also. At least I know that often the genuinely important issues are decided in the small corners of life.

I mention these little incidents of the airport and the phone conversation only because they were the first opening to me of what it meant to respond to the demands of life from the divine Center. But it is this reality that lies at the heart of all Christian simplicity. As we yield to the Center everything about us becomes focused, synoptic. This yielding is nothing more than the experience of the great commandment to love God with all our being. A French Christian, Marie of the Incarnation, wrote in 1628, "My spirit was more and more being simplified. . . . In the depths of my soul . . . these words were continual; 'Ah! My Love, my Well-Beloved! Be blessed, O my God!' . . . And since that time my soul has *remained in its center* which is God."[5]

I hope you understand what I mean when I speak of living out of the Center. I am of course referring to God, but I do not mean God in an abstract theoretical sense, nor even God in the sense of One to be feared and revered. Nor do I mean God only in the sense of One to be loved and obeyed. For years I loved him and sought to obey him, but he remained on the periphery of my life. God and Christ were extremely important to me but certainly not the Center. After all, I had many tasks and aspirations that did not relate to God in the least. What, for heaven's sake, did swimming and gardening have to do with God? I was deeply committed, but I was not integrated or unified. I thought that serving God was another duty to be added onto an already busy schedule.

But slowly I came to see that God desired to be not on the outskirts, but at the heart of my experience. Gardening was no longer an experience outside of my relationship with God—I discovered God in the gardening. Swimming was no longer just good exercise—it became an opportunity for communion with God. God in Christ had become the Center.

Our Many Selves[6]

You may be wondering what all this has to do with simplicity. Perhaps I could explain it this way. Within all of us is a whole conglomerate of selves. There is the timid self, the courageous self, the business self, the parental self, the religious self, the literary self, the energetic self. And all of these selves are rugged individualists. No bargaining or compromise for them. Each one screams to protect his or her vested interests. If a decision is made to spend a relaxed evening listening to Chopin, the business self and the civic self rise up in protest at the loss of precious time. The energetic self paces back and forth impatient and frustrated, and the religious self reminds us of the lost opportunities for study or evangelistic contact. If the decision is to accept an appointment on the human services board, the civic self smiles with satisfaction, but all the excluded selves filibuster. No wonder we feel distracted and torn. No wonder we overcommit our schedules and live lives of frantic faithfulness. But when we experience life at the Center, all is changed. Our many selves come under the unifying control of the divine Arbitrator. No longer are we forced to live by an inner majority rule which always leaves a disgruntled minority. The divine Yes or No settles all minority reports. Everything becomes oriented to this new Center of reference. The quiet evening can be enjoyed to the fullest because our many selves have been stilled by the Holy Within. The business self, the religious self, the energetic self, all are at peace because they know we are living in obedience. There is no need to wave the flag of self interest, since all things good and needful will be given their proper attention at the appropriate time. We enter a refreshing balance and equilibrium in life.

Until we begin to move into this way of living we cannot possibly make sense out of Jesus' startling statement, "Let what you say be simply 'Yes' or 'No'; anything more than this comes from evil" (Matt. 5:37). When all of life's motions are governed by the heavenly Monitor, then we speak and make decisions in simplicity. Before, when asked to lead a campaign for minority rights (or teach a Sunday School class or whatever), our competing selves engaged in vigorous debate. "It's the right thing to do!" "But really now I am just too busy." "The need is so great, and besides think of all those who will approve of the action . . . but then what of those who will disapprove." "And what if I become entangled with the authorities, perhaps thrown into prison." And on it went. We jerked back and forth between Yes and No, indecisive, confused. From earliest days we had been taught that God is not the author of confusion, but there we sat in inward disarray.

But when we live out of the divine Center, thoughts and decisions flow from the Fountainhead. All relevant data are considered, to be sure, but decisions stem from a source deeper than facts and figures. Once we have understood the mind of the Father, we can speak our Yes or No with confidence. We will have no need to reverse our decision if the winds of opinion change, for we have spoken out of a deeper Reality than the latest Gallup poll.

Earlier I spoke of God on the periphery of my life. Actually, it would be more accurate to say that I was on the periphery of his Life. It was I who needed to come into the Center, the Core. It is one thing for God to come into us (and a very necessary thing), but it is quite another for us to come into God. In the first instance we are still the center of attention; in the second God is the focal point. When God comes into us we still have a certain autonomy; when we come into God we have come IN. He is in all and through all and above all. This is no infantile pantheism, as if God could be captured in his creation; it is a marvelous majestic monotheism—one God from whom all life is sustained. It is life out of the divine Center.

The focus of Christian simplicity becomes more clear when we change the image flow from God coming into us to our coming into God. "Christ in you" was certainly an important theme in Paul's teaching, but his favorite and most frequent image was of us "in Christ." In the latter case, Christ has become the reference point and we are making the movement into him. When we are in Christ, truly in Christ, our deeds and words are of one piece, because they both flow from a single Spring.

A Perpetual Communion

You may well ask if such a life is possible. Can we really hear God in such a way that each decision can be ordered and governed by him? Can we live in virtually constant communion with the divine Center of the universe? Can Christ truly be present among his people so that he can be heard? Oh, yes! His voice is not hard to hear. His vocabulary is not hard to understand.

Through his illustrious missionary and literary career, Frank Laubach bore repeated witness to this reality. His diaries and books on prayer are peppered with his many experiments to remain in constant communion with God. On the first day of 1937 he wrote in his diary, "God, I want to give you every minute of this year. I shall try to keep You in mind every moment of my waking hours. . . . I shall try to let You be the speaker and direct every word. I shall try to let You direct my acts. I shall try to learn Your language."[7] What a marvelous resolve for the new year! Three months later, he noted his progress in learning to practice God's presence: "Thank Thee . . . that the habit of constant conversation grows easier each day. I really do believe *all* thought can be conversations with Thee."[8]

Think of the number of people who have been encouraged in this way by the simple writings and profound life of Brother Lawrence. How vastly enriched we are that he was finally persuaded, almost against his will, to write down how he had learned *The Practice of the Presence of God*. His famous words still throb with life and joy, "The time of business does not with me differ from the time of prayer; and in the noise and clatter of my kitchen, while several persons are at the same time calling for different things, I possess God in as great tranquillity as if I were upon my knees at the blessed sacrament."[9] Every thought, every decision, every action stemmed from the divine Root. A simple kitchen monk, who meekly referred to himself as the "lord of all pots and pans," found it to be possible. We can too!

But we fool ourselves if we think that such a sacramental way of living is automatic. This kind of living communion does not just fall on our heads. We must desire it and seek it out. Like the deer that pants for the flowing stream, so we thirst for the living Spring. We must order our lives in particular ways. We must take up a consciously chosen course of action that will draw us more deeply into perpetual communion with the Father.

I have discovered one delightful means to this end to be prayer experiments that open us to God's presence every waking moment. The idea is extraordinarily simple. Seek to discover as many ways as possible to keep God constantly in mind. "There is nothing new in that," you may say. "That practice is very ancient and very orthodox." Exactly! This desire to practice the presence of God is the secret of all the saints. "Pray constantly," urged Paul (I Thess. 5:17). "In everything by prayer and supplication with thanksgiving let your requests be made known to God" (Phil. 4:6). "For all who are led by the Spirit of God are sons of God" (Rom. 8:14). Of course it is not new. Countless millions have shown it to be a practical living reality.

Have you ever tried to live out your day so that you fill each moment with the thought of God? I do not mean that you are to cease normal activity. Oh no! Just the opposite. Bring God into each activity, infusing it with the divine Light.

One night I made a high resolve: every person whom I saw the next day I would consciously try to lift into the light of Christ. In the morning I jumped up, had breakfast, and was on my way to work before I realized I had not prayed at all for the family. One by one I sought to immerse them in the Light. Once at the office I rushed in, gave the day's work to my secretary, and was walking out the door before I realized my omission once again. I prayed for the joy of the Lord to enter her day. By now I was beginning to realize how far my life was from constant communion. I became more collected within. Then as I went through the routine of my day I sought to beam prayers at each one I met. I asked for discernment to perceive what was in people, inviting Christ to comfort those who seemed hurt, encourage those who seemed weary, challenge those who seemed indifferent. It was a wonderfully happy day. Sometimes people I would pass on the street would turn, smile, and wish me a good day.

We can help people immensely in this secret ministry. Once, in an ordinary committee meeting, I felt moved to pray for one member who seemed weighted with sorrow, even bitterness. I, of course, participated in the discussion, but all the time inwardly I sought to bathe this person in the light of Christ. The meeting was somewhat difficult due to her rather caustic remarks, especially toward two others in the group. But as we prepared to dismiss, this person suddenly began to weep and finally said to the group, "I wish you would pray for me." After she had shared the source of her hurt and anger, the two who had been verbally attacked gathered around her and prayed the most tender prayer of healing and release. The room seemed full of power and joy.

Frank Laubach spoke of his "Game with Minutes." The idea is to take a given hour each day and see how many minutes during that hour you can be conscious of God's presence. At first you will find the practice difficult and your "score" will be low. That is all right; you are developing new spiritual muscles. With practice, the habit will become more and more ingrained. Make your first experiment in a worship service and hopefully that will be an aid to your concentration. In time extend the experiment to the whole of your day.

When I first began reading Laubach's journals, I was puzzled by the notations at the top of each day: "Conscious 50% ... Conscious 25% ... Conscious 80%." No explanation whatever was given and I would wonder, "Conscious of what?" Finally I realized that he was playing his little game with minutes and recording the percentage of each day that he felt he was living conscious of God's presence.

I'm glad he called it a game, because it is a delightful spiritual exercise. Besides, there needs to be a certain joyful light-heartedness about our task. Otherwise we will become overly serious and dreadfully boring. Meister Eckhart remarked, "The soul will bring forth person if God laughs into her and she laughs back into Him."[10] Our work is no grim duty. It is a delightful privilege. We are engaged in a joyous adventure, not a sourfaced penance. God is no killer of happiness. In this little exercise we are coming alive to God. Every person, every tree, every flower, every color is alive with God for those who know his language. Kagawa said that every scientific book was a letter from God telling us how he runs his universe.

And the glory of this experiment is that it works best when we concentrate not upon ourselves but upon others. We miss the point if we are taking our spiritual temperature every few moments to see if we are concentrating upon God enough. How much better if we try every moment to give God to someone else. It is wonderful to walk onto a grade school playground and inwardly lift every child into the arms of Christ. Or to ride in the back of a bus and invite Christ to visit with each person that boards. Carpenters and plumbers and electricians can fill the homes in which they work with the light of Christ, praying for each member of the family, or if it is a new home for the family which will live there. Grocery store clerks and retail checkers can pray for each person who passes through the line, imagining him or her drawing closer to God. In my work I write many letters, and so each time I sign my name I try to pray for the person to whom the letter is addressed. It is great fun to imagine the recipient opening the letter and being strengthened with a fresh sense of God's presence. There are thousands of these little experiments you can try, and very often you will be startled by the results.

And most wonderful of all is what happens inside us. More and more we develop what Thomas á Kempis called a "familiar friendship with Jesus."[11] No longer is "Jesus, Lover of My Soul" a quaint song—it is an amazing experience. To our astonishment we find that we are walking with God. His thoughts are becoming our thoughts, his desires our desires. Increasingly, old ugly thoughts melt away and our minds become pure as a mountain stream. Proof upon proof begins to pile up that God is at work in our daily lives, until we become certain of God, not from books or preachers, but from experience. The old strain and indecision are replaced by a greater ease and confidence.

Of all the inward changes we experience, the most awesome is that we begin to know his Voice. We become inwardly acquainted with the language of the true Shepherd. Humbled under the cross, we are able increasingly to discern the true Spirit from the clatter and clamor of human voices, and even the hollow voice of the enemy who comes under the guise of an angel of light. We begin to live in guidance. Inward promptings give unity to our decisions. All the demands for service are somehow filtered through the Light. Our lives are being simplified because we are giving attention to only one Voice, and our Yes and No arise from that Center. We no longer rush puffing and panting through our jam-packed day, yet somehow we accomplish more. Thomas Kelly witnessed, "Life from the Center is a life of unhurried peace and power. It is simple. It is serene. It is amazing. It is triumphant. It is radiant. It takes no time, but it occupies all our time. And it makes our life programs new and overcoming."[12]

The Principle of Contentment

One of the most profound effects of inward simplicity is the rise of an amazing spirit of contentment. Gone is the need to strain and pull to get ahead. In rushes a glorious indifference to position, status, or possession. Living out of this wonderful Center causes all other concerns to fade into insignificance. So utterly immersed was St. Paul in this reality that from a Roman prison he could write, "I have learned, in whatever state I am, to be content" (Phil. 4:11). To be abased or to abound was a matter of indifference to him. Plenty and hunger, abundance and want were immaterial to this little Jew with the Titan soul. "I can do all things through Christ who strengthens me," he said, and so he lived (Phil. 4:13, NEW KJV).

How cleverly Paul turned the tables on all those who taught that "godliness is a means of gain" by replying that "there is great gain in godliness with contentment" (I Tim. 6:5, 6). He saw that the problem with material gain is its inability to bring contentment. John D. Rockefeller was once asked how much money it would take to be really satisfied. He answered, "Just a little bit more!" And that is precisely our problem—it always takes a little more; contentment always remains elusive.

But the wonderful thing about simplicity is its ability to give us contentment. Do you understand what a freedom this is? To live in contentment means we can opt out of the status race and the maddening pace that is its necessary partner. We can shout "No!" to the insanity which chants, "More, more, more!" We can rest contented in the gracious provision of God.

I still remember the day this reality struck me with unusual force. I was passing by some very expensive homes, and began pondering our perennial tendency to want something bigger, better, and more plush. At the same time, I was monitoring the rise of covetousness in my spirit as I admired those homes. I carried on a little inward dialogue. Was it possible, I wondered, to come to the place where you do not desire more house even if you can afford it? Couldn't you decide on a particular economic livability level and rest contented with that, even if your income exceeded it considerably? The response was swift: "Oh yes! It is not necessary to always crave more. You *can* live contented with what you have, with no further desire to accumulate more." I'm quite sure I have not attained this holy contentment, but from time to time I have known a measure of its liberating graces and have found it a wonderful resting place.

Think of the misery that comes into our lives by our restless gnawing greed. We plunge ourselves into enormous debt and then take two and three jobs to stay afloat. We uproot our families with unnecessary moves just so we can have a more prestigious house. We grasp and grab and never have enough. And most destructive of all, our flashy cars and sports spectaculars and backyard pools have a way of crowding out much interest in civil rights or inner city poverty or the starved masses of India. Greed has a way of severing the cords of compassion. How clearly the Apostle Paul saw this when he warned that our lust for wealth causes us to fall into "many senseless and hurtful desires that plunge men into ruin and destruction" (I Tim. 6:9).

But we do not need to be imprisoned to avarice. We can be ushered into a life of peace and serenity. With Paul we can say, "If we have food and clothing, with these we shall be content" (I Tim. 6:8).

I wish I could end our discussion of contentment on this high note. But as you have probably already realized, contentment has certain difficulties. The great problem with a principle of contentment is its tendency to baptize the status quo, to give religious sanction to present conditions. It is the kind of counsel that the powerful enjoy giving to the poor and defenseless. Often it is the very spirit of *discontent* that has prompted wonderful changes for good. There is a kind of holy restlessness that inspires important social advances. And so we are faced with the practical issue of knowing when our disquiet stems from a God-given concern to improve conditions, and when it is the result of self-serving greed. There are, of course, no foolproof answers, but I share the following guidelines in the hope that they may at least turn us in the right direction.

First, we can share the concern with other brothers and sisters whose discernment we respect. Second, if our restlessness has its root in anguish over the plight of those whose condition is clearly desperate, most likely it is of the Lord. Third, if the concern involves the well-being of our children, it is often right. Fourth, if we are wanting to improve our own state, we should not automatically assume that it is wrong. Fifth, let us consider if our discontent has its source in a lack of inward peace with Christ. Sixth, we need to learn to distinguish a genuine psychological need, such as cheerful surroundings, from an obsession. Seventh, we must grow in our discernment between desires that spring from Heavenly Love and those arising from the love of money. Eighth, by an act of the will we must still every motion that is centered in greed.

Moving Up and In

The inner integration I have described is the longing of many. We weary of competing commitments and exhausting schedules. We desire to be obedient to God in all things, and have a growing knowledge that this frantic scramble is not his will. We yearn to enter the deep silences that give unity and force to our service.

Desire, however, is not enough. If we expect to enter the inward simplicity for which we were created, we will need to order our lives in specific ways. The things we do will not give us simplicity of heart, but they will put us in the place where we can receive it.

One way to nurture simplicity is through the discipline of silence. Society is dominated by the inane notion that action is the only reality. Please, for God's sake and your own, don't just do something, stand there! Come in and enjoy his presence. Sink down into the light of Christ and become comfortable in that posture. Open the subterranean sanctuary of your soul and listen for the *Kol Yahweh*, the voice of the Lord. To do so gives us focus, unity, purpose. We discover serenity, unshakableness, firmness of life orientation.

At first we will hesitate to do this. It is strange territory and, as Blaise Pascal said, "The eternal silence of the infinite spaces terrifies me."[13] But if we will once overcome our fear and quiet ourselves we will discover that Christ is our Friend who desires our company. Our fear comes from our unfamiliarity with centering down our lives. In his book *Nurturing Silence in a Noisy Heart,* Wayne Oates says, "Silence is not native to my world. Silence, more than likely, is a stranger to your world, too. If you and I ever have silence in our noisy hearts, we are going to have to grow it.... You *can* nurture silence in your noisy heart if you value it, cherish it, and are eager to nourish it."[14]

Yes, we can have a holy silence within, but we need to nurture it. And when we do, miracles occur. If we are assailed by temptation, all we need to do is quiet ourselves into the power of God and watch the good rise up and the evil dissipate. It is wonderful—this resting in God, this stilling of frantic activity, this seeking first his Kingdom.

At all times, but especially in the beginning, we need to find a specific time and place to nurture silence. As a teenager I used to go out behind the garage and sit on a wall with my feet on the trash cans. It was a quiet sanctuary there, and I learned to commune with the Father. One May day Frank Laubach wrote, "The day had been rich but strenuous, so I climbed Signal Hill back of my house talking and listening to God all the way up, all the way back, all the lovely half hour on the top."[15] Some draw near in the recreating silences of the early morning, others quiet themselves best in the deep quiet of the night, still others retreat from the blast of the day for a time of attentive, listening silence. We must have a time to still the churning, to quiet the restlessness, to meditate on the almighty God who dwells in our hearts.

Another important ingredient in opening the way for interior simplicity is to get in tune with the God-given cycles of life. There are cycles of eating, cycles of sleeping, cycles of work, cycles of play. And when these God-appointed cycles are broken, misery is the result. My students often suffer from a simple denial of the normal cycle of sleep. Large numbers of Americans endure immense heartache (and heartburn) from the failure to respond correctly to the cycle of eating. Finitude is a cycle, the cycle of growing old. And what a terrible burden we place upon ourselves and others in our desperate attempt to stay young. On the other end, of course, children struggle to be twenty-one and hence independent. People are in misery because they are not yet twenty-one, and people are in misery because they are past twenty-one, and that leaves most of us in misery most of the time.

Many of us would find great relief in discovering our own cycles of activity and quiet. For example, I function best when I alternate between periods of intense activity and of comparative solitude. When I understand this about myself I can order my life accordingly. After a certain amount of immersion in public life, I begin to burn out. And I have noticed that I burn out inwardly long before I do outwardly. Hence, I must be careful not to become a frantic bundle of hollow energy, busy among people but devoid of life. I must learn when to retreat, like Jesus, and experience the recreating power of God. We are told that Peter tarried in Joppa for many days with one Simon, a tanner (Acts 9:43). And along our journey we need to discover numerous "tarrying places" where we can receive heavenly manna.

This knowledge is a wonderful freedom. No longer do I rebuke myself that I am not giving enough attention to study and meditation in the days of intense activity among people. Nor do I any longer malign periods of quiet reflection or vacation as unproductive sloth. I can understand and value the hidden preparation through which God puts his ministers. I am free from desiring public gaze when I need hiddenness.

Still another step toward simplicity is to refuse to live beyond our means emotionally. In a culture where whirl is king, we must understand our emotional limits. Ulcers, migraines, nervous tension, and a dozen other symptoms mark our psychic overload. We are concerned not to live beyond our means financially; why do it emotionally? Let us repudiate the modern success image of the person "on the go," whose workload is double what any single person can possibly accomplish. Let us reject the delusions of grandeur that say we are the only ones who can save the world. We must learn our emotional limits and respect them. Our children and spouses will love us for it.

Is there anything more we can do? Yes, much! We can keep a record of all our activities for one month. Then we should rank them in the following way: absolutely essential—number 1, important but not essential—number 2, helpful but not necessary—number 3, trivial—number 4. Next, we must ruthlessly eliminate all of the last two categories and 20 percent of the first two. We are too busy only because we want to be too busy. We could cut out a great deal of our activity and not seriously affect our productivity.

Purposefully, we can cultivate the life of reflection. We need not merely listen to the news or read the paper, we can ponder its significance. Let's get the broad picture on the events of our time and evaluate them. The real prophets of our day are those who can perceive what is happening in modern society, see where it will lead us, and give a value judgment upon it. Let's wrestle with "existence clarification"—who we are and what our purpose for being is. We can take a one-day retreat just to reflect on our direction in life. We should not just absorb facts, but think about their significance. When a brilliant philosopher friend of mine went on a one-year sabbatical, I asked him what he would do. "For the first three months I plan to do nothing but think," was his reply. Most of us cannot be unencumbered for three months, but we can think. Thinking is the hardest work we can do, and among the most important.

Another step that opens us to heart simplicity is the commitment to a previously agreed rule. The covenant of marriage is perhaps the clearest example of this. Think of the host of costly and painful decisions that are avoided by this commitment. No flirting with divorce, no casting about for better options—marriage becomes a *decision* to love and cherish each other until death. In our family we have decided how much per month we will spend on entertainment. That simple commitment greatly reduces the strain and stress of decision-making. I have set a limit on the number of speaking engagements I can accept that will allow me to maintain my other obligations with integrity. When that limit has been reached, I can decline even "wonderful opportunities" with amazing speed, because I feel God has called me to that limit. I have been saved enormous frustration and over-commitment by the simple rule of *never* accepting a speaking engagement over the telephone. By the time a letter has arrived, my enthusiasm has been tempered by realism. A mother or father who has decided to stay at home until the children are school age eliminates many wonderings and vacillations about this or that job. Patterns are, of course, not always perfect, and they sometimes need to be broken, but for the most part they economize greatly the frustration of numerous decisions.

Of all the virtues, simplicity is the most inviting because it brings such inward unity. François Fénelon put it most emphatically: "O, how amiable this simplicity is! Who will give it to me? I leave all for this. It is the pearl of the Gospel."[16]

6. INWARD SIMPLICITY: HOLY OBEDIENCE

The fruit of holy obedience is the simplicity of the children of God.
                              —*Thomas Kelly*

T. S. Eliot speaks of Christianity as "A condition of complete simplicity / (Costing not less than everything)."[1] Holy obedience is stamped with that enormous price tag. Holy obedience is the insatiable God-hunger that will make a person dissatisfied with anything less than the pearl of great price. Holy obedience is the joyful abandon of the person who will sell absolutely everything to buy the field. It is the obedience of an Abraham willing to plunge the knife into his own dear son at the *Kol Yahweh,* the voice of the Lord. It is three Hebrew children who refused to bow the knee to the golden image. It is a Daniel who would die before he would stop praying to the one true God.

Holy obedience is the single eye that bathes the entire personality in light. It is the purity of heart that can desire only one thing—the good. It is a God-intoxicated life that can embrace wealth or poverty, hunger or plenty, crucifixion or acclaim with equal ease at the word of Christ.

Dr. Graham Scroggie, a gifted preacher of another generation, preached on the Lordship of Christ at a huge Keswick Convention in England. A great orator, he spoke powerfully. After the crowd had left, he saw a young college student seated alone. He went to her, asking if he could help. "Oh, Dr. Scroggie," she blurted out, "your message was so compelling, but I am afraid to truly make Christ Lord, afraid of what he will ask of me!" Wisely, Graham Scroggie turned his worn Bible to the story of Peter at Joppa, where God had taught him about his racial and cultural discrimination. Three times God brought down a sheet laden with animals unclean to orthodox Judaism and said, "Rise, Peter; kill and eat." Three times Peter responded, "No, Lord." Tenderly, Dr. Scroggie said, "You know it is possible to say 'No,' and it is possible to say 'Lord,' but it is not really possible to say, 'No, Lord.' I'm going to leave my Bible with you and this pen and go into another room and pray for you, and I want you to cross out either the word 'No' or the word 'Lord.'" He did so, and when in prayer he felt that the matter had been settled he slipped back into the auditorium. The young woman was weeping quietly, and peering over her shoulder he saw the word 'No' crossed out. Softly she was saying, "He's Lord, He's Lord, He's Lord." Such is the stuff of holy obedience.

Going Deeper

We must be more precise, more concrete about this matter of holy obedience. Otherwise it will remain forever a pious-sounding theoretical ideal that does not much affect the way we live. Meister Eckhart wrote, "There are plenty to follow our Lord half-way, but not the other half. They will give up possessions, friends, and honors, but it touches them too closely to disown themselves."[2] As we cross over the line and venture into this second half, we find ourselves in the land of holy obedience. To gladly disown ourselves, to live in joyful self-renunciation, is the other half from which we so often draw back. Jesus declared, "If any man would come after me, let him deny himself and take up his cross and follow me" (Mark 8:34). Harsh demand, this self-denial. We would much prefer more comforting words like "self-fulfillment" and "self-actualization." Self-denial conjures up in our minds all sorts of images of groveling and self-hatred. We imagine that it most certainly means self-contempt and will probably lead to various forms of self-mortification.

What we have failed to see is this amazing paradox: true self-fulfillment comes only through self-denial. There is no other way. The most certain way to miss self-fulfillment is to pursue it. "He who finds his life will lose it, and he who loses his life for my sake will find it" (Matt. 10:39).

It is wonderful, this losing of one's self through a perpetual vision of the Holy. We are catapulted into something infinitely larger and more real than our petty existence. A blazing God-consciousness frees us from self-consciousness. It is freedom. It is joy. It is life.

I cannot stress enough how essential this quality is to true simplicity of life. It is the only thing that will allow us to hold the interest of others above self-interest. It saves us from self-pity. It lifts the burden of concern over having a proper image. It frees us from bondage to the opinions of others.

No one has written with greater vigor or more perception on the connection between selflessness and simplicity than the seventeenth-century Archbishop of Cambrai, François Fénelon. In his sensitive little book *Christian Perfection,* Fénelon identifies three stages through which we travel on our way into the simplicity of self-blindedness. The first stage involves freeing ourselves from an "intoxication" to material or outward things and becoming sensitive to the things of the spirit, especially our own inward condition. We are no longer dazzled by the outward, the superficial. Impressive buildings, bulging budgets, flashy programs simply fail to move us. We give up on all the outward human systems to accomplish the work of God. Our attention is drawn to the more internal work of the Spirit. We become absorbed with the work of God upon the soul. It is a good and healthy step, but deeply self-centered and far from genuine simplicity. "It is a wise self-love, which wants to get out of the intoxication of outside things."[3]

In the second stage we move away from total absorption in ourselves and our eternal destiny to being centered in the fear of God. It is a step forward but it is, as Fénelon said, "a weak commencement of true wisdom," since we are "still wrapped up in self."[4] In this stage it is not enough for us to fear God, we must be *sure* that we fear him. We fear not-fearing. We have a kind of spiritual rigor that is determined to obey God. We are constantly returning to our own behavior to see if we can find any dregs of pride or avarice. There is a great longing for humility, and we work with all our might to attain it. There is a keen sensibility of sin within. A strong identity is felt with St. Paul who, regardless of what others had done, could feel in the depths of his being that he was the "chief of sinners" (I Tim. 1:15).

This stage is one of great honesty and sincerity, but it is not yet true simplicity. "Sincerity is a virtue below simplicity,"[5] said Fénelon. The reason is easy to see. The sincere have a deep concern for honesty and truth. Rectitude, fidelity, conscientiousness, impeccability—these all mark the sincere. And although all of these are great virtues, they have a certain self-consciousness about them: a concern to do right, to be right, to look right. Of the sincere, Fénelon says, "They are always studying themselves, going over all their words and all their thoughts, and going back over all that they have done, afraid of having said or done too much."[6]

The sincere are not yet simple. They have a kind of artificial rigor that makes us feel uncomfortable, though we cannot fault the virtue. They put us on edge and make us feel ill at ease. This often concerns us because they seem so spiritual, so determined to know God. We wonder if our discomfort stems from a resistance to God and his way. In reality, however, it is due to the fact that these deeply committed folk are trying too hard. They lack the ease, freedom, and naturalness that mark true interior simplicity. We would prefer less perfect people who are more at ease with themselves.

This stage in the spiritual walk must never be despised. It is, in a certain sense, necessary as we are coming into God. In the Christian fellowship there needs to be a sufficient measure of grace and latitude to allow our brothers and sisters and ourselves to travel through these experiences. Nor must we hurry people through this stage too quickly. People who see the peace and liberty that comes from simple love often try to push themselves (and everyone else) into it before they are ready. This is a grave mistake. As the wise preacher of Ecclesiastes said, there is a time and a season for everything under heaven, and there must be times of inward struggle and penitence. When the time is right, the spirit is nourished by the bread of careful introspection. There is a proper place for inner disturbance and rigorous examination. Brother Lawrence witnessed to ten years of this inner turbulence.[7]

Having cautioned you about too brief a sojourn in this stage, I must hasten to add that neither must we become too attached to this period, for we are only pilgrims through the land. We were never meant to set up permanent residence there. An inward resting in the midst of strife is the rightful inheritance of the children of the Kingdom (Heb. 4). When God begins to open us to something more pure, we are to follow promptly and never lose time in backward glances.

As we move along, God will lead us into the third stage, in which our attention becomes more and more drawn to the divine Center. "It begins to consider God more often than it considers self, and insensibly it tends to forget self in order to become more concerned with God with a love devoid of self-interest."[8]

Please understand, this is not the destruction of self or the loss of individuality in some sort of "cosmic consciousness." This is the discovery of the self achieved by focusing our attention on the Creator of the self. It is losing the self in order to find it. Only in this way can the true self blossom and flourish.

This third stage is a marvelous virtue, and something sublime. It is the natural charm and unpretentious exuberance of simplicity. We admire people who walk in this way, and enjoy their company. Gone is the forced behavior and sticky righteousness.

Do you know the wonderful new freedom this simplicity brings? No longer is there the stifling preoccupation with ourselves. Now there are new liberating graces to care deeply for the needs of others. And most wonderful of all, we can lay down the crushing burden of the opinions of others. Fénelon witnessed, "With this purity of heart, we are no longer troubled by what others think of us, except that in charity we avoid scandalizing them."[9] We do not *have* to be liked. We do not *have* to succeed. We can enjoy obscurity as easily as fame.

We have also a curious liberty to speak about ourselves, not excessively but naturally. I say "curious" because most people assume that those who are truly unself-conscious would never talk about themselves. That approach belongs to an earlier period in which, out of false modesty, we try to quell any rise of pride. We are afraid that maybe we have said too much. We slip an example or word about ourselves into the conversation and immediately worry that it was inspired by vanity. We determine that we will never speak of ourselves, neither our accomplishments nor our failures, lest in either case *we* become the center of attention. At many points this is indeed good counsel, but it is a strained humility and contrary to simplicity. In time, however, we begin to relax, and are enabled to speak of ourselves with the same candor as we do of others. "Simplicity consists of not having any wrong shame, or false modesty," writes Fénelon.[10]

The Apostle Paul knew this freedom to an amazing degree. He could assert his Roman citizenship and his Hebrew lineage when it was needed. He could boast of his many sufferings for Christ's cause: beatings and stonings, shipwrecks and sleepless nights, hunger and thirst (II Cor. 11:24–29). He received his Apostleship and teaching from Christ alone, and even opposed Peter for his cultural Jewish Christianity (Gal. 1, 2). He was so free and unpretentious that he could boldly urge believers, "Be imitators of me, as I am of Christ" (I Cor. 11:1).

Here is language that most of us would not dare utter. On our lips it would seem like the height of arrogance, and probably that is exactly what it would be. But Paul was beyond such petty self-admiration. He had passed through all that long ago. The hidden preparation through which God had put this man had changed him. We cannot understand the things that Paul said and the life that Paul lived until we see that he had given up on all the little human systems of self-aggrandizement. Without exaggeration he could call it all "dung," because he was living in a greater Power. And when we see ourselves desperately struggling for the "dung," we can be fairly certain that we know little of this "power of his resurrection, and the fellowship of his sufferings, being made conformable unto his death" (Phil. 3:10). Paul knew what it meant to be free from himself. What a desperately needed freedom it is today!

Throughout history there have been various traditions which, in one form or another, have advised verbal debasement of ourselves in order to gain mastery over reigning pride. We can remember this tendency in some of the ascetic practices of the Middle Ages, but it is also in evidence today in what I have sometimes called "worm theology." "Without God I am nothing, I am no good, I am a worm!" Whatever merit such statements have theologically, I honestly doubt that they have much value in increasing selflessness. Fénelon is, I think, far wiser when he says simply, "Self-love prefers injury to oblivion and silence."[11] To be silent is probably the best way to deal with self-love.

In simplicity we are also free to let others speak well of us when it is appropriate. I still remember the day I was with a group of friends and one person paid me a sincere compliment. With self-conscious modesty I blushed, hemmed and hawed, and tried to shrug off the remark. A very perceptive friend in the group looked me straight in the eye and said, "Foster, you don't know how to take a compliment, do you?" That was a turning point for me. I realized that a compliment, if given in honesty and not to impress, should be taken seriously. I had no right to affront people by rejecting their gift of love. Over the years since that incident, God has given me a measure of freedom in that regard, and it is a happy freedom.

In all of this we can sometimes get the mistaken impression of uninterrupted progress forward. Even the use of the term "stages" can unwittingly convey the idea of leaving one level for a higher one never to return again. I have not found it to be so. My experience has been much more fluid and undulating. One day I may be experiencing an intimate attention to Christ's presence that is well nigh amazing, and the next day I am in the "Slough of Despond." I can alternate between being meekly submissive and stubbornly rebellious with surprising speed. And I find many of the devotional masters record similar experiences. The stages are not hard and fast. There is a lot of movement back and forth, up and down.

But it is not a spiritual roller coaster either, because through all the motion there is a sense of progress and growth. The feeling of intermittent communion begins to give way to more sustained fellowship. Whereas before the hard thing was to seek his face, more and more the hard thing is to refrain from seeking him. Slowly and certainly, howbeit with many reversals, knowing God moves from obligation to delight. Although many times we do not pay attention to the holy Whisper, increasingly we do. We are less and less discouraged by our many wanderings in the wilderness because, having tasted the land of promise, we desire it more and more. As much as we may flirt with double-minded living, our real love is singleness of purpose and increasingly it is capturing our heart. We cannot help being drawn toward this way of life when we read the inviting words of our mentor, François Fénelon, "When we are truly in this interior simplicity our whole appearance is franker, more natural. This true simplicity... makes us conscious of a certain openness, gentleness, innocence, gaiety, and serenity, which is charming when we see it near to and continually, with pure eyes."[12]

Joy the Hallmark

Does all this sound difficult to you? Perhaps you are saying to yourself, "I thought I was doing well to get to stage one, and now I discover that it is the bottom rung! It sounds like too much work for me." Yes, it is work—but then again, it isn't. Once we begin, we discover that Someone is working on our behalf, and carrying the bulk of the load. It is the easy yoke and the light burden of which Jesus spoke. The Hound of Heaven is doggedly after us to do us good.

Actually this reality is not something we can bring about by gritting our teeth and fortifying our will. There are things for us to do, as we shall see, but they are more like getting in step with the Leader than blazing the trail for ourselves. There is a quality of yieldedness, a living in the passive voice. Fénelon observed, "The more docile and yielding a soul is in letting itself be carried away without resistance or delay, the more it advances in simplicity."[13]

I often have students who are keenly conscientious and determined to come into God. Sometimes I need to counsel them to relax and quit trying to be so religious. Recently, I had one such student who was struggling desperately and praying fervently over an internal matter. I shocked him when I said, "Please stop praying. You are working at this too hard; let me do the praying for you." Such a small word, and yet it set him marvelously free.

Joy, not grit, is the hallmark of holy obedience. We need to be lighthearted in what we do to avoid taking ourselves too seriously. It is a cheerful revolt against self and pride. Our work is jubilant, carefree, merry. Utter abandonment to God is done freely and with celebration. And so I urge you to enjoy this ministry of self-surrender. Don't push too hard. Hold this work lightly, joyfully.

The saints throughout the ages have witnessed to this reality. Think of St. Francis, the poor little monk of Assisi, inebriated with the love of God and filled with ecstasy. Those early Franciscans walked in holy obedience with the most incredible exuberance and merry abandon. Jubilant, they lived rapt in God by the overflow of divine grace that descended upon them. Juliana of Norwich in her beautiful *Revelations of Divine Love* said that she was filled with "delight and security so blessedly and so powerfully that there was no fear, no sorrow, no pain, physical or spiritual, that one could suffer which might have disturbed me."[14] Blaise Pascal wrote, "Certitude. Certitude. Feeling. Joy. Peace. . . . Forgetfulness of the world and of everything, except God. . . . Joy, joy, joy, tears of joy."[15] And on and on march the witnesses.

You know, of course, that they are not speaking of a silly, superficial, bubbly kind of joy like that flaunted in modern society. No, this is a deep, resonant joy that has been shaped and tempered by the fires of suffering and sorrow—joy through the cross, joy because of the cross.

The Rise of Humility

Of all the theological virtues, humility is one of the most coveted. No one enjoys people who are consumed with themselves. Smug arrogance is always distasteful. Genuine humility, on the other hand, has a gentleness about it that is delightful. There is an unpretentiousness in true humility that all people appreciate.

But humility is as elusive as it is desirable. We all know that it can never be gained by seeking it. The more we pursue it the more distant it becomes. To think we have it is sure evidence that we don't. But there is a way for humility to come into the habit patterns of our lives. Holy obedience opens the door. It is a central means of God's grace to work humility into us.* It is not hard to see how this can be. When the whole of our vision is filled with the Holy, petty selfishness is squeezed out. Perpetual God-consciousness of necessity eliminates self-consciousness. Thomas Kelly wrote, "Humility rests upon a Holy blindedness, like the blindedness of him who looks steadily into the sun. For wherever he turns his eyes on earth, there he sees only the sun. The God-blinded soul sees naught of self, naught of personal degradation or of personal eminence, but only the Holy Will."[16]

For the Christian, this comes as wonderful news. How many times we have longed to be free of our own self-conceit and domineering pride. What needless anguish we have borne simply because we were not noticed. We puff and strut to get a little attention, and later deplore our vanity. Wistfully we have seen the humility of others and ached to know its ease and freedom. How deeply we have desired to obey the word of Scripture to take on the mind of Christ, who though God the Son did not grasp for equality, but rather "emptied himself, taking the form of a servant.... And being found in human form he humbled himself and became obedient unto death, even death on a cross" (Phil. 2:7–8).

How wonderful now to see the connection between humility and obedience. Jesus "humbled himself and became obedient." There is a way into humility, and it is through holy obedience. The God-possessed soul knows only one purpose, one goal, one desire. God is not some figure in our field of vision, sometimes blurred, sometimes focused; he IS our vision. Our eye is single, our whole body is full of light. Selfishness cannot find a toehold.

---

* In *Celebration of Discipline* I mention that the Spiritual Discipline of service is also used by God to bring us humility. Service is, of course, an outflow of holy obedience. This again demonstrates the interdependence of the Disciplines.

First Steps

You may feel that the way of living we have been considering is a quantum leap from your present experience. Not only do you feel that you are in left field; you are in another ballpark, maybe another league. That probably overstates the case, but even if it is an accurate description of your situation you need not be discouraged. You do not have to be advanced in the intricacies of sainthood to begin to move into holy obedience. You do not even need to know all of the problems or pitfalls. You need only one thing: a desire to know God and to walk with him. And even if you do not desire God but wish you did, you may ask him for the desire and he will give it to you. Indeed, I would go so far as to say that the very fact that you are reading this book is desire enough for God to begin bringing the grace of holy obedience into your life.

Holy obedience does not just fall upon our heads. There are things we can do that will draw us into this sacred sanctuary. So I share the following "first steps" but I share them only as suggestions of the direction we need to travel, not as laws to encompass the journey. You can trust God to individualize the teaching: some things he will no doubt urge you to ignore; certainly he will teach you many personalized steps I do not mention. Above all, seek to be attentive to your present Teacher, whether through these words or beyond these words.

The first step I want to give you is not something to do at all. It is something to refrain from doing. Very simply, we should not try to be less egocentric. The attempt would be self-defeating. The more we work at being unconcerned about ourselves, the more conscious of ourselves we become. And so what are we to do? Nothing. Let the matter drop. It is one of those things in life that will never yield to a frontal attack. Concentration upon the problem redoubles its strength. This matter will be cared for in due time, but only if we first forget it and turn our attention to other things.

The second step is rather like the first in that it is less a plan for action and more a call to focus our field of vision. We are to discipline ourselves to "seek *first* the Kingdom of God." This focus must take precedence over absolutely everything. We must never allow anything, whether deed or desire, to have that place of central importance. The redistribution of the world's wealth cannot be central, the concern for ecology cannot be central, the desire to get out of the rat race cannot be central, the desire for simplicity itself cannot be central. The moment any of these becomes the focus of our concern, it has become idolatry. Only one thing is to be central: the Kingdom of God. And, in fact, when the Kingdom of God is genuinely placed first, the equitable distribution of wealth, ecological concerns, the poor, simplicity, and all things necessary will be given their proper attention.

In a particularly penetrating comment on this verse of Scripture, Søren Kierkegaard considered what sort of effort should be done to pursue the Kingdom of God. Should a person get a suitable job in order to exert a virtuous influence? His answer: no, we must *first* seek God's Kingdom. Then should we give away all our money to feed the poor? Again the answer: no, we must *first* seek God's Kingdom. Well, then perhaps we are to go out and preach this truth to the world that people are to seek first God's Kingdom? Once again the answer is a resounding: no, we are *first* to seek the Kingdom of God. Kierkegaard concludes, "Then in a certain sense it is nothing I shall do. Yes, certainly, in a certain sense it is nothing, become nothing before God, learn to keep silent; in this silence is the beginning, which is, *first* to seek God's Kingdom."[17]

And so I urge you to still every motion that is not rooted in the Kingdom. Become quiet, hushed, motionless until you are finally centered. Strip away all excess baggage and nonessential trappings until you have come into the stark reality of the Kingdom of God. Let go of all distractions until you are driven into the Core. Allow God to reshuffle your priorities and eliminate unnecessary froth. Mother Teresa of Calcutta said, "Pray for me that I not loosen my grip on the hands of Jesus even under the guise of ministering to the poor."[18] That is our first task: to grip the hands of Jesus with such tenacity that we are obliged to follow his lead, to seek first his Kingdom.

The third step is so simple I am almost embarrassed to mention it, and yet it is so important that I must. Begin now to obey him in every way you can. Start right where you are, in the midst of all the tasks that press in upon you. Do not wait for some future time when you will have more time or be more perfect in knowledge. The Roman governor Felix wanted to wait for a more "convenient season," but we all know that there is no more convenient season. "Today when you hear his voice, do not harden your hearts," warned the author of Hebrews (Heb. 3:7–8). Right now, as you read these words, ask for an increase of the light of Christ. Ask that the Shekinah, the glorious radiant presence of God, which once filled the mercy-seat, fill your heart. In every task of your day seek to live in utter surrender, listening and obedient.

Allow me to share with you a very small experience, but one that may help you to see what I mean. This occurred at an especially busy time in my year. I was preparing for a weekend trip that involved speaking at three different churches. The financial arrangement was for each church to take up a little offering on my behalf when I had finished speaking. As I was meditating on what God desired of me for that weekend, I had the strong impression that I was not to take any money at all from these churches. For some time I struggled over this directive, for we were counting on the money to meet several obligations. The struggle further revealed an inward greed that I thought had been exorcised long ago. Finally, I felt clear that this was what I had to do if I was to be obedient. I shared this with my wife, for I felt we had to be in unity on the matter. She released the money much more easily than I, noting that perhaps there would be some people in the meetings who needed to know that ministers of Christ were not always after their pocketbooks.

I told the pastors of the first two churches that any offering should be given to the poor or disposed of in whatever way they saw fit. Although surprised at my unorthodox request, they were congenial to the idea. But I arrived at the third church just as the service began, and so had no opportunity to explain my concern. I was relieved, however, when they did not take up an offering for me, and assumed that the matter was settled.

It was late when I finally arrived at the home where I was to stay the night. As I walked in the door my host handed me a check of an amount that was, for me, considerable. It was from the church. I protested, but they mistook my concern for modesty and insisted with such vigor that I let the matter drop.

I wish I could express to you the experience I went through that night. There was the check lying on the nightstand, mine to take. I did not want to cause offense or seem ungrateful; after all, the money had been given for me. Maybe this last church should be considered an experience separate from the others. But what about the earlier directive—it *had* seemed quite clear. Back and forth I went. Finally, I had about decided that I really should take the money rather than cause any trouble, but I determined to review my decision once more in the morning when I was rested. I invited God to teach me while I slept if he desired.

When I opened my eyes the next morning it was unmistakably clear to me that I could not—must not—take the money. A period of meditation only intensified the conviction. With considerable trepidation I explained to my hosts as best I could why I was not able to accept the gracious gift. The moment I finished there rushed into me an unspeakable joy. Though outwardly I tried to remain calm, I was being filled with an overwhelming sense of the glory of God. Once alone in the car I shouted and sang and blessed God. I did not have to be controlled by money! I could live in obedience! It was wonderful, jubilant ecstasy, and although the profuse exuberance lasted for perhaps twenty minutes, the sense of deep warm joy flowed over me all day long. (I was pleased to learn later that the church decided to give the money for refugee work in Cambodia.)

It was such a small matter, and yet obedience was so important, so necessary. And you can obey him right where you are with the light you now have. Begin today, this moment.

A fourth advice in holy obedience is to get up quickly and keep going if you stumble and fall. You will fall, you know. I shared one incident of victory, but I could also tell you of so many times when stubborn self-will would shake its defiant fist at the gentle Voice: times when I simply didn't want to listen so that I would not receive any disturbing instruction; neglect of whispered urgings to visit a neighbor or write a letter.

But when we do fail we do not need to give excessive time

mourning the loss. We need to make confession, get up, and start again immediately. Nor should we linger long at the site of battles won. The issue in holy obedience is not whether we failed or succeeded yesterday or this morning, but whether we are obedient *now*. Does heaven's light blind us to all other affections *now*? Is our eye single, are we living in simplicity *now*?

A fifth counsel in holy obedience is to still all vain talk about ourselves and others. I am not referring to gossip—I'm sure you ended that long ago. I mean the subtle mutual backscratching that is profoundly dishonest, the strokes we give people, not to encourage them but to win them to our side. These over-flattering compliments are seldom thought to be deceitful, but they are. It is not the straightforward speech that Jesus said would characterize the children of the Kingdom (Matt. 5:33–37). And I have discovered that it does not really promote the honest warm relationships we seek. Instead, it places an extra burden upon our brothers and sisters who are truly seeking to know humility of heart and now have to deal with our zealous misrepresentation of them.

In a public meeting I once spoke of a fellow pastor as "the most capable and compassionate pastor I know." Later this good friend confronted me about the statement, saying that he did not feel compassion was yet a distinguishing characteristic of his ministry. He was helping me to see the difference between a true compliment and sheer flattery. A compliment affirms what is already there or coming into being. Flattery degrades us by saying something is that isn't.

We would do well to discipline our words to what is actually the case without embellishment or overstatement. A commending word fitly spoken can be a special benediction, but we need to be careful not to offend propriety.

I shall mention a sixth word of counsel in this walk, which many have found especially helpful. I refer to the practice of keeping a spiritual journal. It is something of a book of remembrances, a personal Ebenezer to say, "Hitherto the Lord has helped us" (I Sam. 7:12).

A journal is immensely encouraging, for we often forget over the years from what petty self-centered depths God has brought us. We tend to be so immersed in the tussle of the moment that we fail to see that the issues over which we now struggle are vastly more significant and substantial. Many matters are settled and behind us.

Beyond this, a journal has the added merit of focusing and concentrating our thinking. Writing out our concerns helps to clarify things and keeps us honest. Self-centered prayers become manifestly self-centered, even to us, when seen on paper. Insights that are hazy figures on our horizon sometimes become crystal clear when committed to a journal. Vacillating indecision can be turned into marching orders.

Many have been helped by sharing their journal notations with each other, thus providing mutual accountability and encouragement. None of us can live in holy obedience on our own. We need the help and encouragement, and even rebuke, of our brothers and sisters.

In our day a great crowd of concerns presses into our little lives, demanding attention. Neighbors are lonely, marriages are floundering, social injustice is prolific, world hunger is escalating. We are pulled, pushed, torn. We need not answer these concerns by rushing out in double-minded obedience. With our eyes blinded to all else by a flaming vision of God, we may respond decisively in holy obedience.

7. OUTWARD SIMPLICITY: BEGINNING STEPS

*There are two ways to get enough: one is to continue
to accumulate more and more. The other is to desire
less.*   *—G. K. Chesterton*

Personal finance is the new forbidden subject of modern society. Once we were afraid to discuss sex in public, but no more. Now we flaunt our newfound freedom like an adolescent first learning to smoke. Then death was the subject no one dared discuss above a whisper. That day is gone too. Seminars on death and dying abound. We can buy tapes, films, and books on how to die gracefully. Gerontology is fast coming into prominence as a major science.

The great taboo today is personal finances. How we spend our money is our business, and nobody is going to tell us what to do with it. Vigorously we resist any public airing of so private a subject. When laws are passed to force public officials to give an open accounting of their stewardship, they still find ways to obscure the truth. Sermons on lifestyle or our obligation to the poor are viewed as a personal affront, a breach of private boundaries. We pull down the shades over our financial affairs; we balance our budgets and shuffle our credit cards behind closed doors.

Today there is a heretical teaching that is an absolute plague in American Christianity. It is the dogmatic and unexamined credo that whatever we gain is ours to do with as we please. If we earn $50,000, how we spend it is our private affair. Perhaps we will concede that it is legitimate for the church to talk about tithing, but the other 90 percent is none of its business.

How utterly self-consumed and provincial! In no way can we

twist the Scripture to justify such a belief. Our lifestyle is *not* our private affair. We dare not allow each person to do what is right in his or her own eyes. The Gospel demands more of us: it is obligatory upon us to help one another hammer out the shape of Christian simplicity in the midst of modern affluence. We need to love each other enough to sense our mutual responsibility and accountability. We are our brother's (and our sister's) keeper.

Precision without Legalism

In attempting to determine what simplicity might look like in the marketplace, we are accepting a massive assignment, one fraught with difficulties. We are now moving out of the realm of interpretation and into the realm of application, and that is always risky business. No longer is our primary question "What does the Bible say?" We must now concentrate on the question, "What does the Bible say to us?" As you know, we have been working on this second question all along, but it now becomes the center of our attention. It is wise to begin such a difficult task by setting forth some foundational building blocks which will undergird our effort.

The first such overarching principle is the necessity of precision without legalism. No one knows more keenly than I the grave danger in giving specific outward application to simplicity. How do you address such a wide variety of people with different needs and vastly different circumstances?

Some have large families, others have small families or no children. Still others are single. Some children have unusual needs that increase significantly the demands of time and money. The needs of teenagers are different from the needs of children.

We come from varying backgrounds. Some grew up during the depression, and felt keenly the evil of too little. Others grew up in post–World War II affluence, and felt keenly the evil of too much. It is not hard to see why the accumulation of possessions would be called prudent by the first group and hoarding by the second.

We are different emotionally. One needs privacy, another

thrives on crowds. One is sensitive to beauty and symmetry, another has no interest in such matters. One person may need a variety of new wallpaper or paint, while another person could not even tell you the color of the living room after five years.

Different jobs make different demands. The president of the university where I teach needs a larger house than I do. He regularly entertains groups of forty to fifty people; I panic if we top six. Some jobs are so publicly oriented that absolute privacy in the home is a psychological necessity.

There is also the problem of personal bias. In issues such as these it is always easy for an author to ride a favorite hobby horse or grind the proverbial axe. At the very least, you can be assured that I am keenly aware of the problem of personal prejudice and desire very much to avoid it.

That is not all. We also have the difficully of the changing culture and world scene. We cannot—we must not—live in isolation from our world. What was a prophetic expression of simplicity in one generation may become only quaint in the next. Time changes issues and we dare not close our eyes to that fact if we hope to be redemptive.

And most dangerous of all is our tendency to turn any expressions of simplicity into a new legalism. How quickly we calcify what should always remain alive and changing. How soon we seize upon some externalism in order to judge and control others. How much we like these nice easy ways to determine who is in and who isn't, who has it and who doesn't.

Is it any wonder that we struggle and strain in an attempt to express exterior simplicity? Unquestionably, this enterprise is fraught with many pitfalls and dangers.

But we must not shrink back from our task. We must risk the danger of legalism, because to refuse establishes a legalism in defense of the status quo. Until we become specific we have not spoken the word of truth that liberates.

The writers of Scripture repeatedly took the risk of being specific. Over and over they fleshed out the meaning of simplicity with frightening precision. The difficulty with such precision is obvious: the specific application to one culture and time is seldom transferable to another culture and time. Peter forbade braided hair and wearing of robes because in his day those things were signs of ostentatious elitism (I Pet. 3:3). Few today would bat an eyelash at the rather ordinary practice of braiding hair, and no one even wears the lavish Roman robe. We understand that he spoke to the particular issues of his day; our task is to discern what constitutes ostentatious elitism today, and speak to that situation.

The Old Testament forbade the charging of interest on loans because it was viewed as an unbrotherly exploitation of another's misfortune (Deut. 23:19). In a world of soaring inflation, the question of unbrotherly exploitation could just possibly go the opposite direction—the person who gives a loan without interest may be the one being exploited. Be that as it may, the issue we must struggle with is how we can care for one another today without exploitation.

The law of gleaning was a compassionate piece of legislation appropriate for the Palestinian agrarian culture, whose principal source of livelihood was small family-owned farms. A tender, gracious command, but totally irrelevant for today. The poor are concentrated in our cities and could not possibly get to the farms to glean the grain. Who would want to legalistically attempt to enforce this divine command today? No, we understand that it was a specific and appropriate application of the law of love in that society. Our task is to discover specific and appropriate ways to care for the poor and defenseless today.

Therefore, let us dare to be specific and at the same time always remember that the exterior expression we give to simplicity today may not be appropriate tomorrow. Our task is to walk the narrow path of precision without legalism.

Accommodation without Compromise

The second principle that will guide our journey into outward simplicity is practical accommodation without ethical compromise. We are dealing with the ancient tension of being in the world without being of it. And this tension has extremely practical implications.

We *are* in the world. The truth of the matter is that our lifestyle *is* affected by the culture in which we live. We may dislike that, chafe under it, but we cannot get around it. For example, I take the bus to work. To do so costs 50 cents per ride or $1.00 a day. That computes to $5.00 a week or approximately $250.00 per year. Hence, the single decision to ride the bus to work amounts to more than twice the annual income of one-third of the world's people. The point is that, while you may shout at me that the average annual income in India is $200.00 or that 900 million people in the world subsist on less than $75.00 a year, you have not helped me much except to increase my guilt. I simply cannot live on $200.00 a year. The very fact that I live in a particular society necessitates a certain economic accommodation to that society.

Now I know that these words go down very hard with purists. They would argue strenuously that we must never accommodate ourselves under any circumstances. They would respond to my little bus illustration that I should live closer to my work, or ride a bicycle to work, or quit my work. I, of course, need to take these counsels seriously, but seldom do people get around the problem. In fact, I find that even those who take a vow of poverty make rather substantial accommodations to the culture in which they live, and I mean that in no derogatory sense at all. Accommodation is part and parcel of what it means to be *in* the world. And there are many practical, economic ways in which we accommodate ourselves to our society: swimming lessons for the children, some new books for Mom, a power saw for Dad.

But we can come to the place where right and necessary accommodation crosses over into wrong and unnecessary compromise. We are not to be *of* the world. And the main problem in the church today is our failure to see where proper accommodation leaves off and where compromise begins.

To know the distinction is admittedly a difficult task. We are vastly different people, with vastly different circumstances, and vastly different needs. Obviously we will never find a clear line of demarcation, but that must never stop us from attempting to help one another know when we are crossing over the line.

This task is enormously complicated by modern media propaganda. When taken as a whole, the media commercials constitute a world view, a rival religious philosophy about what constitutes blessedness. We are told by television that the most idiotic things will make us insanely happy. They may well make us insane, but it is genuinely doubtful that they will ever make us happy.

The purpose of all this media bombardment is to increase desire. The plan is to change "That's extravagant" into "That would be nice to have," and then into "I really need that," and finally into "I've got to have it!"

We are taken in, duped, brainwashed. But it is done in such subtle ways that we do not realize what has happened. We think we are wise because we can easily see through the childish logic of the commercials. But the ad writer never intended us to believe those silly commercials, only to desire the product they advertise. And sure enough we buy, because the commercials accomplish their goal of inflaming our desire.

And most diabolical and manipulative of all is the way in which the same company will manufacture competing products. They know that consumers feel they have power if there is a choice, and that feeling of power will cause them to buy, buy, buy. We love the power of refusing to buy one detergent with its stupid brightening crystals, and instead choose another. The choice, however, was really no choice at all, since both brands were made by the same corporation and were basically the same anyway. The apparent cutthroat competition is usually nothing but a phony war to make us think we are getting a better buy. The intention of advertising is not to persuade the viewer to buy a particular brand of this or that, but to create a consumer mood. More luxurious gadgets, more comfortable sofas, more prestigious cars, more . . . more . . . more. The goal is to increase desire.

We need to make firm concrete moves if we ever expect to counter this massive assault of materialism. To obey St. Paul's command "Do not be conformed to this world" (Rom. 12:2) takes deliberate and sustained effort.

We understand the need for a certain adaptation or accommodation to be in the society in which we live, but we want to grow in our perception of when that turns into conformity or compromise. We seek to be in the world without being of the world.

Voluntary Poverty

Serious consideration should be given to voluntary poverty as an important beginning step into external simplicity. "Why," you ask, "would you list poverty as a potential first step into simplicity? Certainly it is the last, most radical step one would take, certainly not something for the beginner." Quite to the contrary, voluntary poverty can be the easiest step of all. Drastic measures are often less painful, a little like tearing off the Band-Aid quickly rather than pealing it back slowly, painfully. This drastic step can sometimes lance the ugly infection of covetousness more readily than anything else. Nothing can strike at the heart of the love of money quite like severing a relationship with money.

In many other respects it is less difficult. The break with possessions is clear and clean-cut. Gone is the struggle about this or that—all of it is forbidden. You own nothing. How much easier, how much simpler than our world of endless decisions between acquiring and not acquiring. Think of young Francis of Assisi throwing away everything and walking naked down the road. Joyfully he tramped the earth, trusting in God and begging for his food. He was free from any need to work through the knotty problems of stewardship of goods. He had no bothersome budget, bank account, or income tax report. In many ways, poverty is the easiest step of all.

The call to voluntary poverty is not obligatory upon everyone, but it is God's word to some. It was this call that the rich young ruler rejected. But there are many who have accepted it and made it their own.

Voluntary poverty provides a crucial identification with the poor and needy. Toyohiko Kagawa made a profound impact for Christ upon Japan; indeed, his witness rose to worldwide fame in Protestantism. A prolific writer, this brilliant young man lived in Franciscan-like love and poverty in one of the worst slums in Japan. His *Songs from the Slums* is an eloquent testimony of one who walked among the poor as poor himself. And in our day, the simple witness of Mother Teresa of India has had worldwide impact. Her compassionate identification with the sick, starving masses of Calcutta has touched us all. And who could count the untold thousands of faithful servants of Christ that these two examples represent?

On a practical level, voluntary poverty is most easily accomplished in groups, the Roman Catholic orders being the most prominent example. In that way provision is made for the individual by the community, and the individual is freed to fulfill his or her calling without economic considerations. As you know, there are many variations upon this approach by many different groups.

Voluntary poverty does not need to be a lifetime commitment. I know of one couple in Colorado who felt the call of God to give up all their possessions. In a simple act of holy obedience they sold their house and gave away everything. In the process of time they have felt clear about acquiring various possessions, but you can well imagine that their spirit about those possessions can never be the same. Today they own a large house near a state university and rent out most of the house to university students in order to facilitate a ministry among them. We can never know for certain, but it is entirely possible that Jesus' call to the rich young ruler to sell all that he had was exactly this kind of one-time only command.

Never forget that poverty is not simplicity. Poverty is a word of smaller scope. Poverty is a means of grace; simplicity is the grace itself. People can live out all their lives in poverty and never know the grace of simplicity. It is quite possible to get rid of things and still desire them in your heart. But there is also a poverty that can be used of God to throw open the windows of heaven to the fresh life of simplicity. How can we know the difference? We are to live listening, attentive, and open. If the word of command comes, then joyfully we obey.

I would like to give a word of counsel to those who are not called to voluntary poverty: do not despise the call of those who are. In our rush to be prudent and reasonable we can sometimes hinder the word of God. Let us be slow to condemn, slow even to give advice. First let us listen tenderly, patiently. It was said of Jesus that he would "not break a bruised reed, or quench a smoldering wick" (Matt. 12:20). And like him we must be careful lest we trample upon the tender spirit of those who are just learning to hear God, or snuff out their beginning insights. And so prayerfully we listen to see if they have indeed received a word from God. As we learn to walk with the Lord and know his ways, it is seldom difficult to distinguish youthful idealism from the call of Yahweh. Likewise, those who are called to poverty must not reject those who have not received that call.

Finally, I suggest one tiny experiment in voluntary poverty that many of us could do with genuine profit as God prompts us. We can go through our home, find one possession that we value, and consider, "Am I growing too attached to this object? Is it becoming a treasure to me?" Having examined our hearts before the Lord, let us give it away. We must not rationalize by saying, "But after searching my heart I know that it is clearly not a treasure to me, and so I don't need to give it away." If it is truly not our treasure we will not mind in the least giving it away, and if it has become our treasure we will want to give it away for our soul's sake. Also we will pray for the person who receives our little gift that it will be a blessing, and not a hindrance, to his or her walk with God.

Planned Spending

By now we could well be feeling that all this lofty talk of resistance to the consumer mentality and of voluntary poverty completely misses our situation. To be quite blunt, we are trying to figure out how to pay the monthly bills, not whether we should give everything away. We are deeply moved by the wretched squalor of Brazil's 35 million poor, but feel helpless to respond. It is almost all we can do to make ends meet as it is. It seems like every time we turn around the children have outgrown their shoes. Our teenagers "dollar" us to death—"It's only a dollar." Escalating food prices, gas prices, property taxes; we just can't seem to keep up.

And most frustrating of all, we cannot see for the life of us where it all goes. Always there seems to be more month than money. We wonder how in the world the paycheck can slip through our fingers so quickly. What happens to it all?

And that is exactly where we must begin. We cannot hope to deal seriously with exterior simplicity until we know what happened to it all. I am constantly amazed that people do not know where their money goes. If people ask us exactly how much we spent on entertainment or clothes or gifts, could we tell them, not in some round figure, but exactly? If not, we need to find a way to know where our money goes. Most of us would be absolutely astonished at how much we spend in certain categories if we would keep a careful record for one year.

This is the most crucial accountability point in a budget. We will design budgets galore, but have no way to see if we actually keep within that budget. So the first ingredient in planned spending is to know where our money goes. There is absolutely no way we can control it unless we know where it is spent.

If we feel this is a lot of unnecessary work, since it involves so little money anyway, we are dead wrong. Forty years of gainful employment times an annual income of $15,000 would amount to $600,000 for which we are responsible. And that doesn't include any increase of salary. We are accountable for the stewardship of that money. How dare we even think of handling such a tremendous resource without careful records.

We have a very practical way to accomplish this in our home. In our budget book we have twenty separate expenditure categories.* When any money is spent we record what it was and how much it cost in the appropriate category. Simple. Bothersome? Sometimes, but even this simple recordkeeping can encourage us to make fewer purchases.

The second step in planned spending is the development of a budget. A budget is nothing more than making the decision where our money goes. Without a budget we forfeit the ability to make that decision. A budget merely controls how much goes where. It keeps us honest with ourselves.

Of one thing we can be certain: our wants will always exceed both our needs and our funds. If our own egocentric greed does not ensure that, then advertising will. If we allow our wants to determine our buying patterns, the result will be chaos—and

---

* Giving, shelter (house payments, utilities, household items, misc.), food, transportation, medical needs, health insurance, life insurance, education, clothing, house improvements, business expenses, gifts, entertainment, savings, income tax savings, investments, vacations, allowances, special needs, miscellaneous.

considerable debt. A friend of mine who is the president of a credit agency tells me, out of considerable experience, that seldom does he find a couple in financial trouble who have been operating with a well-designed budget.

This book is not the place to go into the details of forming a budget; there are many good guides on the market.[1] I would, however, like to make several observations about the task of budget making.

First, it is almost universally true that in the initial attempt to put a realistic budget onto paper, expenses will exceed income. No budget will ever work until the flow *in* exceeds or equals the flow *out*. Something has to change. And I would suggest that you first look at ways to cut back expenses rather than ways to increase income. This is a time for a couple to experience tears and prayer and tenderness. It is not easy to say No to hoped for vacations or Yes to a smaller food budget. But whatever you do, balance that budget.

Second, never go into debt for ordinary expenditures. An investment is one thing, that new tea set you just can't do without is quite another. Remember, deficit spending will work no better for you than it does for the federal government. Perhaps it is permissible to take out a loan to secure a house, but I can hardly think of anywhere else it would be justified, including the purchase of a car. If you need a car, put it in your budget and begin building the fund until you can pay for the car in cash.

Third, build accountability into your budget. Our system is simple: in our budget book I treat each of our twenty budget categories as if it were a separate bank account. At the beginning of each month I record the allotted "deposit" and then deduct expenditures as they are made. For example, our monthly family budget for clothing is $50.00. The first of each month I record a $50.00 deposit in that category. Then, when the question arises as to new shoes for the kids or whatever, the answer is easy: if there is a sufficient balance in the clothes budget, go ahead; if not, wait. The same holds true in all other categories as well.

Fourth, if you exceed your budget don't be discouraged. At least you know where your money is going and are beginning to have some control over it. You will get better and more realistic as you go along.

Fifth, put the giving of money to Christ and his Kingdom in a different financial frame of mind from other budget items. What I mean is this: most budget items we hope to hold down, but our desire is to see giving increase as much as possible. I have one friend who has a financial goal to always give away more than he spends on himself. So we are to work to decrease our operating budget and increase our giving budget.

Unplugging from the Consumptive Society

The Madison Avenue hucksters are working day and night to squeeze us into their mold. They have launched a concerted effort to capture our minds, and the minds of our children. Christian simplicity demands that we break free of this "thingi-fication." But how do we do it? Here are some suggestions. They are not meant to be rules, for some will speak to your condition and others will not.

First, join the joyful happy revolt against the modern propaganda machine. We need to greet with sarcastic laughter all those patently phony television commercials. In unison the family should shout, "Who do you think you are kidding!" List obviously dishonest ads and boycott their products. Write the networks and companies and let them know what you think of their ads. Help your children to see the attempts of commercials to identify status and prestige with their product. Pray for your children and for yourselves to be protected from the subtle drive to always acquire more. Resist obsolescence. Trinkets are added to products to make you unhappy with the old model. Who in the world needs a new model automobile every single year? Significant safety and efficiency changes occur much less frequently. Why not make a car that would last for the lifetime of the owner? Let the industry know you don't want the costly new design every single year, and urge them to put their money into more meaningful tasks.

Use postage paid envelopes of direct mail advertisers to object to unscrupulous ads. Reject any junk mail you can. Resist all those contests that promise free vacations and dream homes to the winner. Nothing is free! All the people who are buying that product are paying for that $200,000 home and all-expense paid trip to Tahiti, plus the multimillion dollar costs of the contest. How much better to dispense with the contests and have less expensive products that the poor could afford. If enough of us saw the evil of them, we could put a stop to those contests. The only reason companies have contests is that people respond to them. What would happen if next year they had a fifty percent reduction in response to their silly games? At any rate, Christians should have no part in this greedy madness. In every way we can, we must do all we can to refuse to be propagandized.

Second, I propose an exercise which many have found liberating. When you decide that it is right for you to purchase a particular item, see if God will not bring it to you without your having to buy it. I have a close friend who needed a pair of gloves for work. Rather than rush out to the store to buy them he gave the matter over to God in prayer. Although he had not spoken to anyone about this need, in a couple of days someone gave him a pair of gloves. How absolutely marvelous! The point is not that he was unable to buy the gloves; he could have done that quite easily. But he wanted to learn how to pray in ways that might release money for other purposes.

Literally dozens of experiments can be made in this realm. Even the rich can do it. Once a decision is made to secure a particular item, hold it before God in prayer for perhaps a week. If it comes, bless God; if not, reevaluate your need for it; and if you still feel that you should have it, go ahead and purchase the item.

One clear advantage to this approach is that it effectively ends all impulse buying. It gives time for reflection so that God can teach us if the desire is unnecessary. Another obvious benefit is the way in which it integrates the life of devotion with the life of service. The supply of our material needs becomes an exciting venture of faith. What better way to learn to pray for daily bread! One small counsel: it is probably wise to give the money you would have spent on the object to the poor in order to avoid the slightest thought of this as a means of material gain.

Third, stress the quality of life above the quantity of life. Refuse to be seduced into defining life in terms of *having* rather than *being*. Cultivate solitude and silence. Learn to "listen to God's speech in his wondrous, terrible, gentle, loving, all-embracing silence."[2] Develop close friendships and enjoy long evenings of serious and hilarious conversation. Such times are far more rewarding than all the plastic entertainment that the commercial world tries to foist upon us. Value music, art, books, significant travel. If you are too busy to read, you are too busy. Discover prayer as an evening entertainment.

Learn the wonderful truth that to increase the quality of life means to decrease material desire; not vice versa. Close your ears to the ads that bellow their four letter obscenities, "more, more, more!" Listen instead to the life-giving words of St. John of the Cross, "Let your soul turn always not to desire the more, but the less."[3] Richard E. Byrd recorded in his journal after months alone in the barren Arctic: "I am learning . . . that a man can live profoundly without masses of things."[4]

Turn your back on all high pressure competitive situations that make climbing the ladder the central focus. The fruit of the Spirit is not push, drive, climb, grasp, and trample. Don't let the rat-racing world keep you on its treadmill. There is a legitimate place for blood, sweat, and tears; but it should have its roots in the call of God, not in the desire to get ahead. Life is more than a climb to the top of the heap.

Never put happiness at center stage. It is the by-product of a life of service, never the chief end of life. Happiness is not a right to be grasped, but a serendipity to be enjoyed.

Fourth, make recreation healthy, happy, and gadget-free. You don't need an expensive jogging suit to run around the block. Walking, jogging, and swimming are among the best forms of human exercise and they require a minimum of equipment. Get close to the earth with hiking, camping, and backpacking.

The bicycle is a wonderful form of transportation that uses renewable energy. The faddish and expensive sports models are unnecessary, and often too complicated for us to repair. I finally got wise and quit seeking after the ten-speeds and asked God for a sturdy, work-horse model. Now I am as delighted as a child with a new toy. Ride together as a family in the evenings.

Repudiate "spectatoritus." The modern spectator sports programs are obscene in their waste of human and material resources. Sports conglomerates know they have Americans trapped, and so they boldly extend the season with pre-season games, and bowl games, and super bowl games, and post-bowl games, and all-star games! Enough is enough. Don't get me wrong, it is a joy to watch some games; but abject slavery is another thing altogether. Many couples have constant fights because one spouse prefers Monday night football to live conversation. Can you imagine?

Encourage cooperative games and play. Why must winning *always* be uppermost? It is quite possible to have fun without winners or losers. Western society has been seduced to believe that competition is the only way to play. Competition has its place; but cooperation also has its place. Balance is what we need.

Fifth, learn to eat sensibly and sensitively. Reject products shot full of poisonous chemicals, artificial colors, and other questionable means used to produce engineered food. Eliminate pre-packaged dinners. Become sensitive to the whole bio-food chain and eat foods that do not do violence to that balance, such as fruits and grain. Grain-fed animals are a luxury that the bio-food chain cannot sustain for the masses of humanity.

Get in on the joy of a garden, even if it consists of pots in a window sill. Can, preserve, dry, and freeze your foods. Thanks to the faithful efforts of my wife, our children eat dried fruit all winter in place of candy, and like it just as well. With several dwarf fruit trees in a back yard you can have fruit fit for a king.

As much as possible, buy more locally produced foods to save the energy required for transportation. Explore producer and consumer cooperatives. Compost all the garbage you can. Recycle all the items you can. Grow all the fresh food you can.

Eat out less. When you do, make it a celebration. An apple and milk is faster than the fast-food "restaurants" and much tastier, not to mention more nutritious. Go without food one day a week and give any money saved to the poor. Have joyful potluck meals with friends. Buy less food rather than more diet pills.

Sixth, know the difference between significant travel and self-indulgent travel. To begin with, refuse to be conned into believing that you have missed half your life if you haven't seen all the glamour spots of the world. Many of the wisest and most fulfilled people in the world never traveled anywhere, including Jesus Christ. If you do travel, give it purpose. Go beyond the splashy travel brochures with their sights of tinselled affluence, and get to places of anguish and pain and human need. Stay in places that identify with the common people of a country. When Albert Schweitzer visited America, newspaper reporters asked him why he traveled in the third class section of the train. He answered, "Because there is no fourth class!"

Become as acquainted with people as you do with places. Make a genuine effort to communicate; you will be enriched by the experience. Why must we always view folks from other cultures as oddities to be examined? I once saw a man grab the camera of someone trying to take his picture and angrily smash it on the ground shouting, "I am a man, not a picture!"

Seventh, buy things for their usefulness rather than their status. In building or buying homes, thought should be given to livability rather than to how much it will impress others. Don't have more house than is reasonable. After all, who needs seven rooms for two people? Do you live alone after raising a large family? Rather than leaving your spacious home, filled with its wonderful memories, consider inviting another single person or some college students to join you. It just might once again fill the rooms with laughter and ordinary squabbles, and help to ease the loneliness you feel.

Consider your clothes. Most people have no need for more clothes. They buy more not because they need clothes, but because they want to keep up with the fashions. Hang the fashions. Buy only what you need. Wear your clothes until they are worn out. Stop trying to impress people with your clothes and impress them with your life. If you are able to, learn the joy of making clothes. Have clothes that are practical rather than ornamental. John Wesley declared, "As for apparel, I buy the most lasting and, in general, the plainest I can."[5]

Now I know that this matter of fashion is much more difficult for teenagers than for adults. Most adults have come into a measure of inward security, and are no longer so vulnerable to the opinions of others; hence they are free from the need to impress them unduly. Teenagers (and some teenage adults), however, have not yet developed this inner sense of place, and feel keenly the need for acceptance and love. Correct fashion is, of course, a cultural means of inclusion and exclusion. And while we must always be cognizant of the potential evil in this superficial form of judgment, neither should we force our children into positions that will mean unnecessary ridicule. These are matters which we must work through with one another in tenderness and love, teaching and encouraging each other.

Furniture can have beauty and usability without costing the world. There is not a thing wrong with the styles of "early attic" and "late basement." Be creative. Your furniture should reflect you, not some stuffy showroom. Build furniture or refinish good used pieces.

Learn to find bargains. Shop at garage sales and Salvation Army Stores. One caution: sales can be cancerous and inflame a covetous spirit. To acquire an unneeded item at a ridiculously low price is no bargain. Pray for inner detachment before ever venturing out into this world of auctions and sales.

One final word needs to be said. Simplicity does not necessarily mean cheapness. Simplicity resonates more easily with concerns for durability, usability, and beauty. Though I built the beds for our children, we purchased the mattresses, and we chose ones that would last for as long as the boys would live in our home. (And I can bear witness that they were not cheap!) Many items should be chosen to last our entire lifetime and beyond, and should be chosen with great care.

Our task is not easy. Often we will wonder what to do in a given situation. We will struggle for integrity as we feel pressures from all sides. Most likely the greatest and most constant pressures, however, will be to ever acquire, ever possess. As we labor to know what to do in each situation, we would do well to keep before us the astute observation of Mark Twain, "Civilization is a limitless multiplication of unnecessary necessities."[6]

8. OUTWARD SIMPLICITY: LONGER STRIDES

To have what we want is riches, but to be able to do without is power.   —*George MacDonald*

Simplicity is the new necessity of the modern era. Our little planet simply cannot sustain the gluttonous consumption of the wealthy West. Mahatma Gandhi said once that the world has enough for everyone's need but not for everyone's greed. It simply is not a matter of somehow raising the standard of living of the poor of the world to that of the affluent West. America has 6 percent of the world's population and consumes 33 percent of the world's resources. If the rest of the world were to attempt to live on our level of consumption, it is projected that all known world resources of petroleum, tin, zinc, natural gas, lead, copper, tungsten, gold, and mercury would be exhausted in ten years.[1] Even if we made a generous allowance for scientific breakthroughs, we still must confess that our planet simply cannot support the overload were the starving masses raised to our level of consumption. Put simply, the earth cannot afford our lifestyle. No, the answer is clear: we must cut back our standard of living if there is ever to be anything approaching a just distribution of the world's resources.

But that is not all. The imperative of simplicity is further heightened when we couple the call for justice with a compassionate concern for evangelism. Precious lives all over the face of the earth are living without hope. People hungry of heart and weary in spirit are longing for the word of Truth. Two-thirds of the people of this earth have not heard the wonderful news of Christ's liberating Gospel. Are you not moved with the desire to do more than ever before to reach out to help? This is no time for business as usual. Nearly two and one-half billion people stand culturally outside the reach of a Christian witness. These "hidden peoples'" will never be reached through the Church as it now stands. No Christian is within their cultural sphere of influence. We must find new creative ways to reach out to the hidden peoples if we ever hope to fulfill Christ's commission to disciple all nations. Such a task will demand vast outlays of time and resources.

The Covenant that came out of the 1974 International Congress on World Evangelism held in Lausanne, Switzerland, states, "The goal should be, by all available means and at the earliest possible time, that every person will have the opportunity to hear, understand, and receive the good news." Our hearts resonate with this high and holy goal. But it will never be realized without drastic and sacrificial lifestyle changes. The Covenant continues, "We cannot hope to attain this goal without sacrifice. All of us are shocked by the poverty of millions and disturbed by the injustices which cause it. Those of us who live in affluent circumstances accept our duty to develop a simple life-style in order to contribute more generously to both relief and evangelism."[2]

Ecologists and economists shout out to us that simplicity is a new necessity. The great host of hidden peoples shout out to us that simplicity is a new necessity. Will we hear their cry?

The Gift of Giving

Wealth is a dangerous thing. The entire biblical tradition underscores that truth. Therefore, I know that the proposal which I will now make is a risky one, but one which is also deeply rooted in Scripture. There are those who are called to the ministry of money. The gift of giving is a vital and valid spiritual gift, and essential to it is the task of using money for the common good. Jesus told us to make "friends of the mammon of unrighteousness" (Luke 16:9, KJV); that is, make Kingdom use of material goods. It is a much needed ministry among us.

Simplicity always calls us to a simple lifestyle, but it does not always call us to a reduction in income. God calls some to increase their income in order to use it for the good of all.

Again, I emphasize the danger of this ministry. We are dealing with dynamite. Wealth is not for spiritual neophytes; they will be destroyed by it. Only the person who has clean hands and a pure heart can ever hope to handle this "filthy lucre" without contamination. Gluttony, pride, greed, covetousness, and avarice can slip in unawares. This path is fraught with great frustrations and temptations, and those who walk it have to face perplexing decisions and tragic moral choices that most people will never have to consider. In many ways our life will be immensely more complex, though it does not need to be complicated. We will need the prayer and support of the people of God who must stand by us, counsel us, guide us. We will be living close to hell for the sake of heaven.

The most subtle and dangerous aspect of the ministry of money is the false sense of power it gives. We begin to feel in control. Others begin to seek us out, not because of who we are, but because of what we have. They begin to look to us in spiritually destructive ways. In one important sense money *is* power, and we have the power to determine the future of this project or that cause, and they know it. And most destructive of all, we know it. Spiritual pride rears its ugly head as the thought seeps in that we are in charge, we call the shots. The degenerative slide continues until a new pseudo-saviour has been born.

Only veteran soldiers can take up this work successfully. Only those who have been disciplined under the Cross qualify. That is why I waited for this chapter to discuss the ministry of money. This is no beginning step, no easy work. Only one skilled in spiritual warfare should ever attempt it. A person is needed who can receive $50,000 from the hand of God one day, and at the divine prompting give it all away the next. (I did say *all* of it, not just a tithe.)

I would never ask anyone to take up this important and hazardous ministry without the aid of spiritual guidance. Clement of Alexandria counseled that the wealthy servant of God should never attempt to work out his salvation alone, but rather should seek advice of a spiritual director. I concur wholeheartedly.

Choose someone or some small group with whom you can share intimately, someone wise in the things of the Spirit—a person who is not impressed by money, and able to speak the word of Truth with tenderness. Seek his or her counsel and advice. Share your spiritual goals, including a detailed accounting of your financial goals. Be open, listening, teachable. If he or she detects in you a spirit of possessiveness and shares that with you, do not become defensive. Listen eagerly to these words of life. You desperately need this help. The work you have undertaken puts you in constant spiritual danger. It is entirely possible to become disqualified from this high holy work.

But it is a wonderful work. Immense good can come of it. I think of innumerable servants of Christ who quietly and unpretentiously have been the channel through which huge sums of money have flowed. Released from any need to hold on to or control it, they have been able to freely receive and freely give.

The historically rich building in which I write this book was constructed in 1886 as Garfield University. Massive stonework and beautiful turrets give it a castle-like appearance that can be seen for miles around. But in 1897 it was empty and deserted. It was then that James Davis read the advertisement offering the defunct campus for sale, and said to his wife, "Anna, I believe this is our chance to give a college to the world."[3] That is exactly what he did. He bought the magnificent building and then gave it to the Quakers for the development of a Christian university. Think of the thousands of lives that have been enriched simply because one man was free to make Kingdom use of material goods! And think of the innumerable places this story can be retold, with a thousand variations, throughout the world, wherever faithful people advance Christ's Kingdom through the ministry of money.

Does it sound to you as if I am speaking only of the wealthy, who out of a vast financial store underwrite great enterprises throughout the world? They have their place, to be sure; but the ministry of money is more often expressed in more simple ways. This work is usually engaged in by ordinary people with limited budgets. The requirement is not great resources, but a humble willingness to be an unhindered channel.

Here is one simple "wineskin" for this ministry. Together the family prayerfully decides on the budget for that year. It is lean, trim, realistic. Provision is made in the budget for retirement and other similar concerns. Included in the budget is a tithe on the budget. Then any money which comes to us in excess of that budgeted figure is given in its entirety to Kingdom purposes. In this way God can trust us to be an unimpeded conduit. We can be the joyful channel for God's resources. The money may come through salary or it may come in completely unexpected ways. We will marvel that God is using us, trusting us.

As a young man, John Wesley calculated that twenty-eight pounds a year (about $65) would care for his own needs. Since prices remained basically the same, he was able to keep at that level of expenditure throughout his lifetime. When Wesley first made that decision, his income was thirty pounds a year. In later years sales from his books would often earn him fourteen hundred pounds a year, but he still lived on twenty-eight pounds and gave the rest away.[4] Wesley, of course, was single much of his life and never had children, so he did not deal with the financial problems engendered by a family; but the idea is a sound one. We can do the same thing. Obviously we have to make adjustments for growing children, savings for college, and inflation, but the principle remains firm.

Here is another wineskin. If both the wife and the husband desire to work, discipline yourselves to live on one salary and give the other away. In this way, one couple could potentially support an entire missionary family. Why not? What better investment opportunity could there be than that? Think what would happen to the worldwide missionary enterprise if each Christian couple would determine to give every second salary to missions.

Try still another model. Take a careful look at your income. Are there ways to so simplify your lifestyle that you can live on half of what you make? If so, rather than quit your job so that your earnings drop to half, plan to give away half of your earnings.

Here is still another approach. Rather than just giving the money away, invest it for the Kingdom of God. It is usually best to set up a separate checking or savings account. Money put into this account is to be used entirely for Kingdom causes.

Then, as you are led, invest the money in ways consistent with Christian principles. The total earnings are either reinvested or given away. At all times hold firm to the policy that the money, including any and all earnings, belongs entirely to God. Investments consistent with Christian principles can be a terribly complex matter. I am not just referring to items that are obviously unchristian. The deeper issues of justice, ecology, and violence must be considered. What about real estate investments that have little regard for a proper stewardship of the earth? What about a company's tie to the military industrial complex? What about corporations who have links to repressive and unjust regimes abroad? Some companies oppress the poor, others pollute the environment, and on it goes. As I noted earlier, the ministry of money is fraught with complexity.

The ministry of giving is a good context in which to consider the tithe. While tithing is not a New Testament measure for giving, it can sometimes be a helpful starting point from which to begin giving. In the early days, the Church of the Saviour in Washington, D.C., struggled with the place of the tithe as one of their corporate disciplines. They sought the counsel of theologian Reinhold Niebuhr, who suggested that they commit themselves not to tithing but to "proportionate giving, with tithing as an economic floor beneath which you will not go unless there are some compelling reasons." As a result, the discipline to which they all now agree reads, "We covenant with Christ and one another to give proportionately beginning with a tithe of our incomes."[5]

This approach has one wonderful advantage: it has a minimum discipline which is not intended to become the standard. All members know the starting point, but understand it to be only the beginning of the journey. Individually and corporately they must wrestle with what it means to give proportionately. That is no small issue. Elizabeth O'Connor has stated the difficulty well when she writes:

> Proportionate to what? Proportionate to the accumulated wealth of one's family? Proportionate to one's income and the demands upon it, which vary from family to family? Proportionate to one's sense of security and to the degree

of anxiety with which one lives? Proportionate to the keenness of our awareness of those who suffer? Proportionate to our sense of justice and of God's ownership for those who follow after us . . . ? The answer, of course, is in proportion to all of these things.[6]

With all of its difficulties, this grace of giving is a happy ministry. So much good can be done. So many lives can be helped. Stanley Mooneyham tells of his visit to the small village of Singhali, in India, a village suffering from a severe drought that plagued that region. He spoke with one Moslem landowner whose well was nearly dry. Though this man was facing disaster himself, he continued to share his water with Moslem and Christian alike. When Stanley Mooneyham told him that through World Vision's relief funds his well would be deepened, his speech stopped in mid-sentence, and he stood with mouth open. "No words came, but his soul spoke richly through the pools which formed in his eyes. With no attempt to wipe them dry, he just stood there and sobbed. He clutched my hand and would not let go. In his eyes I saw the response to love—and his response was love also."[7]

The Gift of Service

A simple lifestyle can also open to us vast new areas of service. It becomes possible to cut back our needs drastically so that we can devote time to important tasks. John Woolman cut back his business ventures in order to give attention to a traveling ministry. He said, "A way of life free from much entanglement appeared best for me, though the income might be small." Though he had several business offers, he refused them all because of the "outward care and cumber" that would divert his energies. Remember, Woolman was not a professional minister in the sense of being free from the concerns of the marketplace in order to preach. He was a businessman, and that was how he earned his living. He simply determined to "live on a little" in order that "nothing might hinder me from the most steady attention to the voice of the true Shepherd."[8]

Many do the same today. One professional carpenter I know

supports his family by working two days a week. The rest of the week is then devoted to the cause of justice for the poor in the city. A citrus rancher friend of mine sold his ranch at such a profit that he and his wife were able to serve for many years on the mission field without any expense to anyone. (They did this later in their lives, after the children were grown.) Many teachers keep their needs pared down enough so that they do not have to earn money in the summer, and can devote their time to ministry among the poor and needy. Many families engage in extensive weekend ministries at considerable expense to themselves in both time and money. And on it goes.

The possibilities are limitless. Many opportunities open up when we believe they are possible. Some situations do not allow us this flexibility, but many more than we think will. We are close to a family who gave this idea a try. The husband is a construction superintendent, and they have the normal responsibilities that come with four children. Over a period of time they began to sense the call of God to give help to a Christian work in New Guinea. Prayerfully and tactfully, the husband was able to arrange for a two-month leave of absence. To be quite honest, the venture involved a considerable expenditure of their personal money in order for the family to be involved in this two-month ministry. And yet the value for all concerned was enormous, well worth the investment, they told me. They are now listening to God to see if they should involve themselves more extensively in the New Guinea work.

One does not need to go to New Guinea, of course. Free time for service is desperately needed anywhere there are people. Crisis centers, counseling services, hospitals, all need our help. The ordinary ministry of local churches could be greatly enhanced if numerous members were free to invest their lives in the work. In one metropolitan city a small fellowship was able to find homes for some 350 homeless children. But to do such things demands a substantial investment of time, and some of us need to find ways to release ourselves. In our day many need to rearrange their lives in specific ways if they hope to engage in the ministry of service.

However, we must not concentrate exclusively upon the financial aspects of service. It is commendable to pare down our needs in order to release time to serve, but Christian simplicity adds another important ingredient. With self-interest rooted out, we have become free to serve as servants. Self-righteous service is banished. We do not have to lord it over others or make them feel indebted to us. Service can be rendered freely and without manipulation. We can joyfully surrender our own rights for the good of others. This is a great liberty in the work of service. It gives us the ability to prefer one another in love.

I would like to give one specific word of counsel in the context of the ministry of service. I think it is important that we find specific ways to serve our neighbors. We need to experience the ministry of small things for those who live near us.

Why would I mention such an insignificant matter? The answer is that it is far from insignificant. To be content with a life of simple goodness among our neighbors demands a total reorientation of values. It involves a whole restructuring of our perspective about what is important in life. Only the grace of simplicity can inform us with that perspective.

To value our neighbor does not put us in the headlines of any publication. It does not give us any advantaged position at work. It is not even valued in many churches, simply because it takes time away from important ministries there. To rake our neighbor's leaves, to babysit their children, to take the time to visit with them is the stuff of service to our neighbor. And until we learn to live in simplicity we will find it hard to believe it is an important ministry. John Woolman spoke of being "weaned from the desire of outward greatness."[9] Without that weaning process we will not know simplicity, nor will we find much place in our lives for our neighbors.

The Gift of Sacrifice

There is a need today for what I call prophetic simplicity. We need voices of dissent that point to another way, creative models that take exception to the givens of society. Obviously, prophetic simplicity runs the risk of excess; but the danger is no greater than the excess of the status quo.

Often these men and women speak to us in hyperbole and exaggeration. We label them hopelessly utopian and idealistic.

All the same, we need their word to jar us loose. Our consciences need to be pricked by their sharp barbs. We need to understand the relevance of their impossible ideal.

Prophetic simplicity is often expressed in ways that make many of us uncomfortable: models that are certainly not obligatory upon all Christians at all times. And yet they are not in opposition to the way of Christ either. They become open windows and swinging doors onto new options, new possibilities. They are participants in the ministry of sacrifice.

Our temptation to reject prophetic simplicity out of hand must be held in abeyance. After all, John the Baptist *is* in the Bible. And although Jesus did not go in much for animal skins and wild honey, that does not mean we shouldn't. At the word of God Elijah lived by a desert stream for three years, and we may be given a similar call. At the heart of prophetic simplicity is self-renunciation for the cause of Christ.

Some have chosen the single life in order to advance the Kingdom of God. In our day many have faulted the Apostle Paul because he urged the unmarried to consider the single life as a genuine option (I Cor. 7). They miss the profound wisdom in his counsel. Marriage of necessity divides one's loyalties. To be faithful to the marriage covenant, the husband and wife must concern themselves with a whole host of personal and financial matters. The single person can concentrate with abandon on the advancement of the Kingdom of God. Every married person with any kind of sensitivity understands very well that this is the case.

Paul was not against marriage, but he did insist that people should count the cost. No one should enter the covenant of marriage without understanding the immense amount of time and energy involved in making that relationship work. We need to face the fact that we cannot do many of the kinds of things which Paul did and be married.

One of the great tragedies of our day is the number of Christian leaders who have given themselves unselfishly to the cause of Christ, but have destroyed their marriages and their children in the process. And it was all so unnecessary. Many of them simply needed to understand that their sense of call was incompatible with the responsibilities of marriage, and to choose the single life. Paul's caution has the ring of practical wisdom. Jesus Himself said that some have become eunuchs for the sake of the Kingdom of God (Matt. 19:12).

We do people a disservice when we fail to proclaim the single life as a Christian option. Marriage is not for everyone, and we should say so. A single person can venture into forms of simplicity that are closed to the rest of us. By word and deed the Church should encourage these faithful servants of Christ. They should never be looked down upon or viewed as somehow odd. We should do all that we can to be with those who have chosen the single life, because they need our friendship and we need their wisdom.

Others who are married have voluntarily chosen to go without children. To be sure, some have made the decision from purely selfish motives; but others have done so in order to be free to care for the children of the world. I am very close to a couple who have consciously chosen not to have children so that they may have a more effective ministry among teenagers. Their home is open to young and old day and night. Although one night in their home is enough to drive me crazy, I must confess that their ministry is an extraordinarily effective one.

A couple must be in covenant unity with one another in any decision of this nature. This is no place for a husband to try to exercise some kind of "headship" over the wife. Such a decision takes time. The feelings of each spouse must be given full expression. At no time should there be conveyed a sense of spiritual inferiority if children are desired. This is a matter of calling, not spirituality.

Most couples will want and should have children, but again we should know the commitment that entails. We must be prepared to pay the financial and emotional price.

Perhaps some will remonstrate, "I wish that I had counted the cost, but I didn't. I now have a family, but still feel called to a ministry that does not have time for marriage and family obligations." I answer that your calling is now to your family. You are to fulfill the covenant made with your spouse. To jump into some kind of ministry that ultimately would be destructive to your marriage is sin. Be content to invest your life in your spouse and your children. If the ministry is important, God will either raise up others to do it, or in his time will arrange your situation so that this work is compatible with your family responsibilities.

Another aspect of the ministry of sacrifice is in the area of Christian fasting. Many have advocated a weekly fast as a means of releasing funds for the world's hungry. This practice is in every way commendable, but I want here to deal with fasting on a deeper level.

Fasting helps to give us balance. It makes us more keenly sensitive to the whole of life, so that we do not become obsessed with our consumer mentality. It is something of an inner alarm to help us hold our priorities straight, to give us a sense of spiritual sensitivity.

Fasting reveals the things that control us. We cover up what is inside us with food and other good things, but in fasting these things come to the surface. The first truth that was revealed to me in my early experiences in fasting was my lust for good feelings. It is certainly not a bad thing to feel good, but we must be able to bring that feeling to an easy place where it does not control us. So many attitudes strive to control us: anger, pride, fear, hostility, gluttony, avarice. All of these and more will surface as we fast. It is a blessed release to have these things out in the open so that they can be defeated, and we can live with a single eye toward God.

The central idea in fasting is the voluntary denial of an otherwise normal function for the sake of intense spiritual activity. Remember, there is nothing wrong with these normal functions in life—it is simply that there are times when we set them aside in order to concentrate. Viewed from this perspective we can see the reasonableness of fasting, and also its broader dimensions. For example, there is a great need today to learn to fast from people. Most of us have a tendency to devour others, and usually we get severe heartburn from it. I suggest that we experience times of fasting from people not because we are antisocial, but precisely because we love people intently and when we are with them we want to be able to do them good, and not harm. Thomas Merton said, "It is in deep solitude that I find the gentleness with which I can truly love my brothers. . . . Solitude and silence teach me to love my brothers for what they are, not what they say."[10]

We also need to have times when we fast from the media. It is amazing to me that many people are incapable of going through an entire day concentrating on one thing. Their train of thought is constantly broken by this demand or that interruption. The newspaper, the radio, the television, magazines—everything interrupts their concentration. Some people are so enslaved to television that if it were taken away they would go through withdrawal. Obviously, there is a time for the various media, but there is also time to be without them.

We can also learn to fast from the telephone. This instrument is a wonderful invention, but it controls many people. Some people will stop praying in order to answer the telephone. Can you imagine anything more absurd? I want to let you in on a secret: we do not need to answer that gadget every time it rings. We are not its slave, but its master. When people come to visit us, we should not insult them by interrupting our conversation to answer the telephone. In our home, when we are eating or when I am reading stories to the children, we do not answer the phone. I want my children to know that they are more important than any phone call. People will call back if they genuinely need to reach us.

Earlier I dealt with voluntary poverty, but I now would like to take up one further aspect of it, namely communalism. Communalism is nothing more than the renunciation of private ownership for the sake of the wider community.

Throughout history, utopian movements have arisen and disappeared in the same way that many ruthless competitive societies have arisen and disappeared. Permanence is not an important criterion; faithfulness is. Many have attempted communal living and found it terribly complicated; others have found it liberating. As a prophetic model for our day it probably allows for the simplest standard of living. Goods that would normally serve one nuclear family can now accommodate perhaps two dozen people.

Although communal approaches to life have existed for many centuries—the most notable being the Roman Catholic monasteries—there has been a recent surge of interest by Christian groups in this expression of faithfulness. The Word of God community in Ann Arbor, Michigan, Reba Place Fellowship in Chicago, Illinois, and the Church of the Redeemer in

Houston, Texas, are a few of the better known examples. The reasons for this revival of interest are not hard to discover. The feelings of alienation and loneliness, the concern for ecological responsibility, the desire for a just distribution of the world's resources, and the joyful freedom to share resulting from the charismatic renewal are a few of the causes. We should also recognize that the size and shape of the nuclear family makes communal arrangements more feasible and desirable. It was not so many years ago that large extended families were commonplace. When you have parents with half a dozen children combined with grandparents and another extra person or two thrown in, you have a community of considerable size and complexity. Today's family of three or four often gains a great deal from sharing with others.

Communal arrangements have many difficulties: how to provide for privacy, how to handle money matters, how to discipline children, and so on. And although communalism has a great deal of historical precedence, there is not much biblical basis for it. Perhaps the greatest value of the Christian commune is its symbolic importance. Quietly, it questions society's affluence, and points to another way.

Identification with the Poor

Another way in which simplicity takes outward shape is through conscious identification with the poor and forgotten. Jesus Christ did so repeatedly, and so must we. The exact expression of our identification will have infinite variety, but there is no doubt that we ought to engage in this loving work.

Many of us need to champion the cause of the oppressed, witness to their misery, and call for justice. We are to plead their cause before the powerful. The Christian is to be the voice of the voiceless, the face of the faceless, before authorities. Is this not precisely what Moses did before Pharaoh? When we represent the poor before the powerful, we are ambassadors of Christ. Quakers on the American frontier would often attend treaty negotiations between the federal government and the Indian tribes in order to plead for justice. Jacques Ellul says, "I hold that in every situation of injustice and oppression, the

Christian—who cannot deal with it by violence—must make himself completely a part of it as representative of the victims."[11]

But a warning is needed here. The Christian must advocate the cause of those who are truly poor and forgotten. So often it seems as if Christians have a particular knack for joining causes that are nearly over and championing issues that have thousands of champions. We must go beyond newspaper accounts (in fact, newspapers are usually a hindrance in this work) to find the genuinely dispossessed. If we desire to identify with the poor we will be concerned to be informed, really informed. Ellul reminds us that Christians "must be so concerned about human misery that they take pains to discover the really lost before it is too late."[12]

This is a thankless ministry. We are seeking to be led by the Holy Spirit to the truly abandoned and defenseless. We will defend the cause of people who are not politically "interesting." We will be bringing before mayors and city councilmen issues that all others would like to sweep under the rug. We will be making people uncomfortable over matters they deem "trivial." But that is what is asked of us if we are to identify with the genuinely poor and forgotten.

Another way we identify with the poor is to be among them. There are some who are led to take this up as a vocation: living among the poor, suffering with the poor, praying for the poor. Albert Schweitzer lived this vocation in Africa as did Toyohiko Kagawa in Japan.

Many of us, however, will be called to be among the abandoned of the earth in less dramatic ways. We will respond to Divine promptings to visit prisons and hospitals, rest homes and mental institutions. We will tutor little ones deprived of basic skills. We will take time to play with the child down the street that sits on the curb alone.

Our children need to join us in this ministry of identification. We do them no favor by hiding them from suffering and need. If we imprison them in ghettos of affluence, how can they learn compassion for the broken of the world? So, let us walk hand in hand with our children into pockets of misery and suffering.

One specific means of identification with the poor is discovered in our approach to education. Do we see a college education, for example, as a ticket to privilege or as a training for service to the needy? What do we teach our teenagers in this matter? Do we urge them to enter college because it will better equip them to serve? Or do we try to bribe them with promises of future status and salary increases? No wonder they graduate more deeply concerned about their standard of living than about suffering humanity.

As we seek to follow in the steps of Jesus, we will be drawn to identify with the poor. As we do, perhaps a valuable question to keep before us is whether we are as willing to evaluate our living standards by the needs of the poor as we are by the lifestyle of our neighbors.

Reachable Handles

It is entirely possible that you have found this chapter extremely frustrating, maybe even irrelevant. Grand ideas of giving and serving, celibacy and communal living, have left you in the dust. You are not certain that you desire those things, let alone do them. I too have felt, and do feel, the same way.

We must not despair that we are still in the foothills. The heights are seldom scaled in a single bound. And so I close this chapter with some practical handles that are within reach of us all.

First, develop a habit of plain honest speech. Strike "I am starved" from your speaking vocabulary. It is not true and obscures the fact that many indeed are starving. When you are hungry say that you are hungry and reserve the word "starvation" for the real thing. Make honesty and integrity the distinguishing characteristics of your speech. Reject jargon and abstract speculation, the purpose of which is to obscure and impress rather than to illuminate and inform.

We have simplicity of speech when our words come from only one Source. Søren Kierkegaard wrote, "If thou art absolutely obedient to God, then there is not ambiguity in thee and ... thou art mere simplicity before God. ... One thing there is which all Satan's cunning and all the snares of temptation cannot take by surprise, and that is simplicity."[13]

Second, write out a money autobiography.* Consider the place of money in your childhood. What view of money did your parents have? Did you feel deprived or privileged? How are those influences affecting you today?

Consider your changing attitudes toward money over the years. What influences have affected the change? Have the changes been good or detrimental?

Consider your own feelings. Are you fearful of the future? Is money a security to you? Do you feel guilty about the money you spend?

Consider your personality. Are you a "nothing ventured nothing gained" person or a "better safe than sorry" person? How does that influence your approach to money?

Third, find new creative ways to get in touch with the earth. Revel in the infinite variety of colors around you. Listen to the birds—they are God's messengers. Walk whenever you can. Enjoy the texture of grass and leaves. Grow flowers or plant trees and discover once again that "the earth is the Lord's and the fullness thereof" (Ps. 24:1).

Fourth, learn to enjoy things without owning them. Possession is an obsession in our culture. If we own it we feel that we can control it; and if we control it, we feel that it will give us more pleasure. The idea is an illusion. Many things in life can be enjoyed without possessing or controlling them. We gain great benefit from "common ownership" of many things: schools, public buildings, parks, rivers, public beaches, roads. Let's learn to enjoy the beauty of the beach without the compulsion to buy a piece of it. Many things can be shared among neighbors or friends. Some cultures even have common ownership of land. Many agricultural kibbutzim of Israel are successful and efficiently run. Give some things away just for the freedom it brings.

Fifth, develop the habit of homemade celebrations. There is an infinite variety of things you can do. It is great fun and draws you closer together. Talk to each other; even little ones can tell the most entertaining stories if we will listen. Read

---

*The concept of a money autobiography is considered in some detail in Elizabeth O'Connor's *Letters to Scattered Pilgrims* (pp. 28–30). I have taken the idea from that source.

books out loud to each other. Such times together make the entertainment extravaganzas of modern society seem cheap and hollow by comparison, and they are.

Invite neighbors and other lonely folk to join you—they won't bite! And please, do not make such a fuss over having guests in that you drop exhausted at the end of the evening and determine never to do that again. How can you enjoy people if you are always trying to impress them? Genuine hospitality is more simple, more relaxed.

Sixth, teach your children by word and deed about the varied aspects of simplicity, including the use of money. In regard to expenditures, draw clear, hard lines beyond which you will not go. Our culture is training them to desire everything in sight when they enter a store. You do them no favor when you give in to their incessant demands. You must protect them, tenderly, firmly. Spoiled children need discipline, not pampering. It is a terrible disservice to fail to set the limits. Get them what they need, not what they want; and in time they will come to want what they need.

Provide your children the experience of a growing self-government. Our children receive an allowance in order to give them the experience of managing money. (We pay twice their age—the six-year-old gets 12 cents per day, the nine-year-old gets 18 cents per day.) But they have to work for that money. They lose 5 cents for every job left undone, though they cannot go below zero. We also decided that it was important for the boys to have jobs they did because they were a part of the family and for which there was no pay. Each child has three banks—one for spending, one for savings, one for giving away. They are required to save 10 percent and give away 10 percent: the rest we decide together how to spend. Presently I pay for their necessities, they pay for their luxuries. In time I will hike up their allowance and go half with them on necessities; eventually they will pay for everything themselves. As we work to give them a growing self-government, our hope and plan is that by the age of sixteen each boy will be managing all his own income and expenses, except for housing and food. By the time they are eighteen, we hope that they will have had enough counsel and experience to make wise and responsible use of their money. (And we hope that we will be wise enough to keep our hands off their decisions, refraining even from giving advice unless it is sought.)

We have no ideal arrangement. Even now we sometimes fight over what is a luxury and what is a necessity. We make many mistakes, but our desire is to help them grow in their understanding of money and its proper use.

Seventh, seek to obey the counsel of John Woolman, "Silence every motion proceeding from the love of money."[14] The love of money is a tricky thing—often those who have it the least love it the most. Watch for that rise within that signals danger. When it comes, be still in the power of God until it is defeated. Do not try to argue down the desire; be silent and quiet. Allow the ocean of love and light to overcome the ocean of greed and fear. If you remain hushed and calm in the grip of Christ, you will discover the good rising and the evil receding.

In attempting to hammer out the outward expression of simplicity, we are undertaking no small task. It will be easy to make mistakes in both restraint and excess. Perhaps the counsel of William Penn will help us to cut back our margin of error: "Frugality is good if Liberality be join'd with it. The first is leaving off superfluous Expenses; the last bestowing them to the Benefit of others that need."[15]

9. CORPORATE SIMPLICITY: THE CHURCH

*I have felt tender breathings in my soul after God
... and strong desires have attended me that his
family, who are acquainted with the moving of the
Holy Spirit, may be so redeemed from the love of
money and from that spirit in which men seek hon-
or one of another, that in all business, by sea or
land, they may constantly keep in view the coming
of His Kingdom on earth as it is in heaven.*
—John Woolman

While individual effort is good, it is always limited. There
are things that we can do together that we cannot possibly do
alone. God has so arranged human life that we are dependent
upon one another to come into all that he desires of us. We
need each other's help in order to know how to love God. We
need each other's help in order to know how to love our neighbor. Lone Ranger Christianity is a contradiction in terms.

In the twelfth chapter of Romans, Paul sets forth a lovely
picture of a community of people living in simplicity. Placed in
the context of teaching on the gifts of the Holy Spirit, Paul
provides a profoundly practical understanding of how we are to
live. We are to give freely to the needs of the saints and to
practice ordinary hospitality. We are to enter into the needs of
one another—rejoicing with those who rejoice and weeping with
those who weep. We are to deal with class and status distinction to the extent that we can freely be among the lowly. We
are to surrender the need to have our own way, and instead
concern ourselves with what will build the fellowship. We are to
live in peace and harmony, never avenging ourselves, always
trusting in God. What an inviting paradigm of simplicity by
which to conjugate our lives!

The Teaching Ministry of the Church

One of the most urgent needs in the contemporary struggle for simplicity in the church is the ministry of teaching. There is a dismal ignorance of the simplest truths about both inward and outward simplicity. People need to know the truth if they are to be set free by the truth. Those of us in the congregation can make a valuable contribution in this direction by encouraging our pastors to dare to address such subjects. We can let them know that we are personally struggling with what it means to be a responsible citizen in a hungry world, and would welcome their instruction and insight. By our own honesty and openness we let our pastor know our willingness to have him or her deal with controversial issues. We are willing to be challenged at the point of our own vested interests, because we desire truth more than our vested interests.

This encouragement can be most helpful. Pastors do not enjoy declaring unpopular messages any more than the rest of us. How encouraging to know of even a few who would welcome thoughtful, prayerful truthgiving.

Pastors also need to take courage and share boldly and tenderly. People need the truth. It does them no good to remain ignorant. They need the freedom that comes through the grace of simplicity. And if we are to bring the whole counsel of God, we must give attention to these issues that enslave people so savagely. Martin Luther is reported to have said, "If you preach the Gospel in all aspects with the exception of the issues which deal specifically with your time you are not preaching the Gospel at all."[1] Given the contemporary milieu, several dimensions of simplicity seem to me to need careful attention in the teaching ministry of the Church.

We must boldly teach the essential connection between the inner and outer aspects of simplicity. We can no longer allow people to engage in pious exercises that are divorced from the hard social realities of life. Nor can we tolerate a radical social witness that is devoid of inward spiritual vitality. Our preaching and teaching needs to hold these elements in unity. If our teaching is centered in the biblical text, we will find literally hundreds of examples—from Abraham to St. John, from the wisdom literature to the apocalyptic writings.

By now you may have grown weary of my constant stress upon this matter, but the need for such a holistic message today is as obvious as the lack of it is terrifying. It is by far the most distinguishing feature of the classical literature on this subject, and the most lacking feature in the contemporary literature. Take, for example, Francis de Sales' *Introduction to the Devout Life,* which has instruction on meditation, prayer, humility, and solitude combined with counsel on wealth, poverty, attire, and simplicity of speech. Or consider William Law's *A Serious Call to a Devout and Holy Life,* which has three chapters on economics set in the middle of a discussion on devotional exercises. Or think of Richard Baxter's *A Christian Directory,* which gives practical instruction on prayer and faith, love and submission, as well as condemning the sin of oppression and boldly setting forth a scheme of economic ethics. This superb balance in the ancient writings between the inward and the outward, between devotion and action, is epitomized so well in the words of Bernard of Clairvaux, "Martha and Mary are sisters."[2] In fact, one of the best ways to help us see the fundamental connection between interior and exterior simplicity is to study in our churches some of the classical Christian writings on this theme.

A second theme that needs to be taught in our churches is the biblical and theological foundations for justice. The message of the prophets must be given new attention. Are we willing to have the scathing social critique of Amos applied to our day? Can we listen to Isaiah's impassioned plea on behalf of the poor and defenseless? Will we give attention to Micah's thundering denunciation of injustice and corruption? Are we willing to hear Jonah's call to worldwide citizenship and missionary responsibility? To hear the biblical message on justice, really hear it, will drive us into the contemporary problems of hunger and poverty.

Another issue that needs earnest study and teaching is the missionary obligation of the Church of Jesus Christ. Despite numerous church mission conferences, there remains a tragic lack of knowledge in this field. Missionaries need to quit boring us with technicolor travelogues and plunge us into an understanding of the theology of missions, the sociology of people movements, and the anthropology of cross-cultural evangelism.

Nothing could motivate us to simplify our lifestyles more than a clear understanding of our responsibilities to the many "hidden cultures" of the earth that have no Christian witness.

A fourth issue that demands thoughtful study is the relationship between simplicity and peace, or conversely, between covetousness and war. Does our luxury and wealth accumulation sow the seeds of revolution and desolation? To what extent is military might used to protect the privileged position of the wealthy, and keep the poor out of the profit-making cycle? Is peacemaking the natural outflow of simplicity? These and many similar questions need careful and prayerful thought.

In our ministry of teaching we also need to rethink our doctrine of work. The goal of work is not to gain wealth and possessions, but to serve the common good and bring glory to God. Even the Puritans, who have often been accused of espousing an unhappy work ethic, saw work as an opportunity to enhance the public good rather than gratify selfish ambition. The great Puritan divine Richard Baxter urged the choosing of an employment in which we could be the most serviceable to God. "Choose not," says Baxter, "that in which you may be most rich or honorable in the world; but that in which you may do most good, and best escape sinning."[3]

Simplicity takes vigorous exception to both the slothful and the workaholic. Diligence and faithfulness are to be praised, but slavish addiction is sin. Simplicity calls us off of a lifestyle of go, go, go. And if we are to teach this reality of unhurried peace and power, we had better demonstrate it in the life of the Church. If we believe in family solidarity, we had better find ways to help families to be together in the evenings rather than in twenty-five different committee meetings. Such frantic hyperactivity is sin, and we should be willing to say so. To be spent in the cause of Christ is a very different reality from the frenzied activity of the modern Church.

If we are serious about teaching Christian simplicity, we will have to address the prevalent theology of wealth. This theology takes many forms, but its point is always the same: God will bless us materially beyond our wildest dreams. This teaching does contain an important truth—God does indeed want to bless his children. The real issue, however, is the purpose for which God blesses us. God's blessing is not for personal aggrandizement, but to benefit and bless all the peoples of the earth. To understand the distinction makes all the difference in the world. The theology of wealth says, "I give so that I can get." Christian simplicity says, "I get so that I can give." The difference is profound.

The fatal flaw in all these little schemes, in which we give to Jesus in order to get rich from Jesus, is the same as that in "chain letters"—someone has to pay. In a world of limited resources, our wealth is at the expense of the poor. To put it simply, if we have it, others cannot.

The Sacred Cow

I have often pondered the perennial desire for bigger and better in the church. I do not say that this is bad, but I wonder about it. I listen, as I am sure you do, to the radio and TV evangelists' constant appeals for money. I receive, as I am sure you do, numerous letters describing the wonderful work God is doing through them, and appealing for more money to increase this good work. Always God is leading these groups to ask for more. I want to speak this tenderly because, quite frankly, I am not saddled with the responsibility of raising vast amounts of money, but isn't it possible that sometimes God would lead us to ask for less? Just once I would like to hear a Christian leader say, "Folks, God has been good to us in many ways, and as we were praying over the future, it seemed as if he desired us to tell you to take the money that you would normally give to us this month and give it to the poor." Isn't it possible that God would lead in this way at times? Such an idea sounds naive, I know, and clearly it is not an effective fund-raising technique. But then obedience is a higher priority than any program or budget, and the advancement of Christ's Kingdom is of greater consequence than our little projects.

I must also give a word about our fund-raising techniques. It is one thing to inform people of legitimate needs; it is quite another to purposely calculate emergency appeals so as to gain the largest response. It is one thing to teach about the spiritual necessity of giving; it is quite another to make use of psychological techniques that are proven to increase giving but have no regard whatsoever for the spiritual state of the individual. It is one thing to help people understand their responsibility for justice and evangelism; it is quite another to persuade and cajole and manipulate the emotions.

Christian fund raising has reached the end of its tether after it has adequately informed us of the need. Convincement is the proper terrain of the Holy Spirit, and we dare not abrogate his work. To be quite honest, I will no longer read appeal letters that have the appropriate sentences underlined in red, and promise to give me a special trinket if I give, and enclose a hand-written (though printed) final note of appeal just in case I have decided to say No. It is with sadness that I refuse to read them, because I am certain that they are often for very good causes; but the approach has moved from information to psychological manipulation.

In our concern for simplicity of speech, I would also like to raise the matter of the naming of our church buildings. There is, I think, an inherent honesty in naming our facilities after the town or street where they reside. All our descriptive adjectives such as "Open Bible" or "Full Gospel" imply that everyone else is "closed Bible" or "half Gospel." Besides, a name such as Maple Street Episcopal Church or Salem Baptist Church helps give us an identity and commitment to the area to which we seek to minister.

I would further caution us in the naming of our fellowship groups. A person once asked me what we called a little group to which I belonged that was attempting to experience a deeper sense of community. I answered, "I think we had better have the reality before we try to name it." I soon discovered that this response was particularly appropriate, as this individual belonged to a group called "Unity House," which had known anything but unity.

I know that naming is a way of describing the distinctive emphasis of a group, but I am concerned that we do not claim more than we can possibly deliver. The usual pattern in the Scripture is to give a new name to someone after his or her transformation has occurred.

Simplicity in speech also deals with the issue of titles of distinction. On this matter Jesus was straightforward: "But you are not to be called rabbi, for you have one teacher, and you are all brethren. And call no man your father on earth, for you have one Father, who is in heaven. Neither be called masters, for you have one master, the Christ" (Matt. 23:8–10).

Does this mean that we can never use the term "father" even in reference to the male parent? Of course not! What Jesus was pointing to is the destructive way we use titles to control and manipulate others. If the rabbi (or professor, or doctor) said it, no one can dispute it. The practical wisdom in Jesus' words is so easy to see in academic institutions. When professors are having a particularly difficult time convincing students, subtle appeals to technical knowledge and advanced degrees usually silence all discussion. Such manipulative control is inconsistent with Christian simplicity. Obviously, some people have more authority to speak on some issues than others, but I have found that that authority has precious little to do with titles of distinction.

It is one thing to teach respect for elders and those in authority, it is quite another to manage and maneuver people by our titles of Doctor, Reverend, Professor, Your Honor, and so on. The title "Reverend" is singularly inappropriate. The term means "one who is to be revered," and that is a distinction that belongs to God alone.

Christian simplicity does not demand a slavish use or disuse of titles. What it does demand is a careful examination of the spirit in which we hold one another, and a willingness to be servants in word as well as in deed.

Aesthetics and Utility in Creative Tension

Any attempt to deal with simplicity in the church cannot avoid the issue of buildings and architecture. This is not an issue that yields to an easy answer, but I would propose that we must hold the concerns for aesthetics and utility in creative tension.

I imagine my little principle is not a very helpful guide to a building committee that is trying to hammer out the size and shape (and cost) of a new sanctuary, but I do think that it can provide some guidance. We need to be concerned for both usefulness and beauty, efficiency and artistry.

In the final analysis, our decisions about architecture and buildings will be determined by our theology of the church, and that is a topic far beyond the scope of this small book. But I present the following suggestions as one attempt to hold aesthetics and utility in creative tension.

One question to answer is the function we want the building to have, since form should always follow function. If worship and adoration is the central concern, then the form articulated in stone or wood or concrete should address that idea. If the primary concern is fellowship, then a different kind of architecture is appropriate. The high arching ceiling is more conducive to adoration, the circle more suggestive of fellowship.

A second suggestion is that we face with brutal honesty the issue of whether our building project is for prestige or the glory of God. I heartily recommend to any group planning to build that they meet together *as a group* for worship and adoration with the single purpose of listening to God about the proposed plan.

I learned the value of this experience in the first building program in which I was involved. It was actually a rather small project—an educational unit that was to double as a day-care center. We had all the right reasons for needing such a facility. We had gone through all the appropriate committees. We had the architect's drawings and had even launched a fund drive. But at that time I was also learning many things about the work of prayer, and finally realized that this was a matter over which we should pray together *as a people*. A meeting for worship was called for that purpose. We met with no pressure to make a decision, for we already had official church approval for the project. We read Scripture, we prayed, we sang, we shared, we listened quietly. It was a wonderful experience. I went into the meeting thinking that probably we should build, and left certain that we should not. The crucial turning point came when I saw the driving force behind my desiring that building to be my unarticulated feeling that a building program was the sign of a successful pastor. Theologically and philosophically, I did not believe that, but as we worshiped the Lord, the true condition of my heart was revealed. Eventually we decided against building, a decision now validated by hindsight.

And so we must find ways to ask if our projects signal money, success, and prestige or service, caring, and the glory of God. "But people won't come unless we dazzle them," you remonstrate. Perhaps, but remember that cuts both ways: many (myself included) will not go to a church that is purposefully trying to dazzle them.

Another suggestion is to call for a revival of the artisan and craftsman. Perhaps someone in the fellowship can carve a beautiful door or altar to the glory of God. Paintings, mosaics, tapestries can be made with care and prayer by fellow worshippers. Sculptures and pottery can be created *soli deo gloria*.

Still a fourth suggestion is to remember that beauty is expressed in many ways other than brick and stone. Flowers and grass and majestic trees can all enhance our sense of color and symmetry. I have often strolled through the Spanish Missions of California and marveled at the lovely quadrangles with their gardens and fountains. If we value fellowship, then we should provide quiet places of beauty and color where friends can sit and visit. Often a tranquil fountain can quiet our inner rush, and drown out street noises as well.

Extravagant you say. Perhaps, but then maybe it is an extravagance that has a kinship to the spilled spikenard of Mary.

Of course, we need to consider the matter of what will fit the geographic and cultural context of the area. And then there is the important issue of cost efficiency. Further, there should be concern for quality and durability. Also, we will want to ask if our facilities are encouraging a lifestyle consistent with the life and teachings of Jesus. These and many more issues grow out of the creative tension between aesthetics and utility.

The Care of Souls

Probably the most significant lack in modern church life is in the ministry of eldering. When Paul gathered the Ephesian elders at the Aegean port of Miletus, he told them to watch over the flock of God which the Holy Spirit had given to them (Acts 20:17–35). This ministry of watching over one another in love is as important now as it was then. Christian simplicity is advanced through the ministry of eldering.

The first thing that must be done if we are to take this work seriously is to provide settings where it can happen. Caring for one another in most churches is quite impossible, simply because we don't know each other well enough to help. A pastor cannot possibly hope to provide adequate shepherding care to a group of any significant size. The answer is for people with the spiritual gift of eldering (whether officially designated as such or not is of little consequence) to give oversight and counsel to the people of God. But elders must get to know their flock if they hope to provide spiritual direction. The class meetings that John Wesley instituted provided this kind of oversight. Converts were divided into small groups that met weekly for mutual accountability and support. Many churches have formed "care groups" or "mini-churches" with the same concern in mind.

What does all this have to do with simplicity? The answer is easy to see: we cannot enter simplicity of life without the help of one another. We need the benefit of people with insight and discernment. For example, there are some people that really need to take a sabbatical leave from their labors in the church. But they will never do it unless someone tenderly urges them to take this step of simplification. Others need to be encouraged out of their sloth and self-interest.

In the early days of Koinonia Farm, a wealthy woman expressed an interest in joining. Clarence Jordan, the founder and spiritual leader of Koinonia, told her to first dispose of her money. "How?" she asked. Jordan replied, "Give it to the poor, give it to your relatives, throw it over a bridge—but you must enter the fellowship without it." She asked if she could give the money to Koinonia Farm. Perceptively, Jordan saw the danger of that act. He accurately discerned her to be a lonely person, lonely because every friend she had was after her money. "If you put that money here," said Jordan, "you would think we courted you for your money and that we loved you for your money." The wealth would become a further barrier to fellowship, Jordan noted, because she would begin to view herself as the great benefactor of the group and feel that they should forever feel indebted to her. Jordan concluded "For your sake and our sake, you get rid of that money and come walk this way with us."[4] What a beautiful example in action of a wise and discerning eldership.

Please do not read these words in too structured a way. I am not dealing with a rigid church policy, or giving license for some demigod of an elder to lord it over everyone else. This is something much less formal and authoritarian. I am only suggesting that we should find ways to receive the help and counsel of those who are endowed by God with the spiritual gifts of discernment and wisdom.

One way many of us have found to allow this gracious ministry to occur is through what is sometimes called "meetings for clearness." They are nothing more than bringing together people whom we respect for their spiritual wisdom, and sharing a matter in the desire to gain "clearness." The issue can be anything from employment decisions (my decision to move from the pastorate to college teaching and writing came out of a meeting for clearness), to sharing budgets for mutual evaluation, to a decision about marriage, or any number of other items.

A decision does not need to be made in the meeting; in fact, it is often best to wait a bit to see if any direction sensed in the group experience is confirmed. An individual shares his or her concern, and then together the group seeks to understand the mind of Christ in the matter. There are questions and discussion, but also prayer and worship. Advice should never be given in haste, lest it distract from the truth rather than lead into it. Words should arise out of the power of God in the midst of the group. Every individual must have the inward discipline to never, never, never interject merely personal bias. People who cannot control their tongue do not belong in such a gathering.

What happens? Often—not always, but often—there begins to emerge a clearer, more certain sense of direction. There is, certainly, the normal sense of assurance that comes from mutual evaluation, but something more occurs—something that does not easily yield to sociological cataloging. It is a reality that I have never known in the ordinary experiences of gathering data, evaluating, discussing and voicing opinions. I have no way to validate it conclusively, but I wonder if the difference is not in the fact that when Christians gather with a commitment to hear the voice of Christ, they receive the direction for which they seek.

Such a group experience can help us keep our eye single. Christian brothers and sisters may warn us if we are taking on too many activities, or if we are getting too puffed up, or both, as one friend said to me once, "You need to lay low in the Lord." They may encourage us that we are moving in the right direction. They may stir us up to love and good works.

The group can also be the catalyst for ministry, and provide a basis for emotional and even financial support. When the word of the Lord came to the "meeting for clearness" at Antioch instructing Paul and Barnabas to go to the Gentiles, they did not need to go to twenty churches to drum up support. The fellowship at Antioch was their base of support: spiritually, emotionally, economically (Acts 13:1–3, 14:27–28).

Suppose in your congregation there is a widowed woman with two small children.[5] She works as a lawyer and is actively involved in your church. But a conviction grows within her that she is to use her profession as a ministry among the city's poor. She calls a group together to help her discern the Lord's will in the matter. What will such a decision mean? First, because of the time commitment of this proposed ministry, she would have to resign from the choir and the nominating committee. Second, the loss of salary would mean that she could no longer give to the church budget as generously as before. Third, and perhaps most crucial, she would experience such a drastic cut in pay that financial assistance would be necessary if she were to engage in this ministry. What happens? Any group which confirms her sense of call would also be committed to helping her find the means for it to happen. Sometimes the group can carry the entire support of the work, other times they become the catalyst for involving others. In either case it is astonishing how often impossible dreams become realizable when a group of people, even a very small group, genuinely believe God is directing them.

The care of souls is an ancient and time-honored ministry. May God grant us new "wineskins" for its fulfillment in our day.

Economic Equipoise

The Apostle Paul set before Christians of all generations a challenging economic principle in his efforts to gather an offering for the poor Christians at Jerusalem (Rom. 15:25–27). He saw the situation in Jerusalem as a wonderful opportunity to express Christian brotherhood across cultural and racial lines.

What a rare privilege for Gentiles to show Christian love to their Jewish brothers and sisters who were in need. Paul spent no small effort to bring this mission of mercy to pass, and we catch important glimpses into it in his second letter to the Corinthians.

He first cites the heartwarming response of the Macedonian believers who recently had been through severe financial difficulties themselves, and still had given with great liberty and joy: "For they gave according to their means, as I can testify, and beyond their means, of their own free will, begging us earnestly for the favor of taking part in the relief of the saints" (II Cor. 8:3).

Here was lavish joyful giving. No mechanical tithe, no calculated attempt to give the least possible amount. They were delighted for the opportunity to share. And Paul encouraged the Corinthians to "excel in this gracious work also" (II Cor. 8:7).

Do you sense the spirit of joy and abandon? This was no time to worry about investment plans and financial security. Here was an opportunity to help Christians in need. Here was an opening to follow in the steps of Christ who, "Though he was rich, yet for your sake he became poor, so that by his poverty you might become rich" (II Cor. 8:9). Only a fool would fail to seize so wonderful an opportunity.

But I have yet to mention Paul's most shocking statement: "I do not mean that others should be eased and you burdened, but that *as a matter of equality* your abundance at the present time should supply their want, so that their abundance may supply your want, *that there may be equality*" (II Cor. 8:13–14, emphasis mine). What an astonishing principle for modern ears. In essence, Paul is suggesting a certain economic balance among the Christian community. It is, as he put it, "a matter of equality." Now Paul is not seeking some kind of precise financial leveling. Gospel liberty was too deeply embedded within him for such pharisaical gymnastics. But he is pointing to a generosity of life that cannot rest in abundance while others suffer in need. Extremes of wealth and poverty are a scandal to Christian brotherhood. They must not be allowed.

To buttress this principle, Paul cited the story of the miraculous feeding of the children of Israel with manna: "As it is written, 'He who gathered much had nothing over, and he who gathered little had no lack' " (II Cor. 8:15).

This Old Testament reference is particularly instructive. Each morning, God graciously provided the children of Israel a supply of the mysterious flake-like material called manna (Exod. 16:9–36). To deal with their insatiable greed and to teach them trust, God commanded that only one-day's supply was to be gathered. True to form, however, some gathered more than allowed; but amazingly, when it was measured with the four-pint omer, "He that gathered much had nothing over, and he that gathered little had no lack" (Exod. 16:18). But some never learn, and they decided to ration out the day's supply so that they could build up a little security for tomorrow. After all, God might not provide them with manna tomorrow. Actually, it was quite prudent and frugal of them. But God wanted to teach them about daily bread, so the stored manna "bred worms and became foul" (Exod. 16:20).

The lessons of the manna were clear: trust God implicitly, no hoarding permitted, and—most pointed of all—no greed allowed. *There were to be equal portions for all.* The reason for equal portions is so practical: it eliminates the occasion for covetousness, jealousy and division. And it is this principle of equality that Paul stresses so vigorously.

What should the principle mean for us today? Inequity in the Christian fellowship is so blatant as to need no demonstration. Millions of our Christian brothers and sisters in Asia, Africa, and Latin America barely escape starvation—many do not escape—not to mention their lack of health care and education. Dare we sit back in our comfort and ease, debating the color of our padded pews, while this scandal exists?

No, of course we must do something. But the real difficulty is exactly how to respond to the problem. Is the early Franciscan fidelity to "Lady Poverty" the best approach? Some have said Yes and have called the church to a radical divestiture of holdings. Some churches may be called to such a step, but many will not. For those who do not feel total divestiture is right for them, I offer three suggestions.

First, we could establish as a budget policy a goal of giving as much to others as we spend on ourselves. I know that this has many difficulties. Is the salary for a Minister of Evangelism giving to others? Is a VBS budget that reaches many new children giving to others? What about a building program that may open the way for many new members? As difficult as the idea admittedly is, still it is a policy worth considering. If nothing else, it would continually force us to ask how much we care about the needs of Christians in other places.

Second, we could develop an ongoing relationship with an economically poor church. This might be an inner city church, or one in another country. When I pastored in Southern California, we developed a relationship with a fellowship in the Los Angeles inner city. When we gathered a "collection for the saints in Los Angeles," we actually appointed people who would take it to them in person. This recommendation also has difficulties. It becomes easy to think of ourselves as God's guardian angel for the other congregation, and expect them forever to be grateful to us. But given all of its dangers, it can still provide benefit to all concerned if done with sensitivity.

Third, we could set aside one special year as a Jubilee, in which we try to give all we possibly can to a particular work. Perhaps we might choose the churches of the Sudan Interior Mission, or the Evangelical Church of India, or our denominational mission program. Individuals may adopt families or local churches. For one year we find as many ways as possible to give as much as possible. Some may sell property holdings, others will have garage sales, still others will sell their car. For one year the budget committee will make an unprecedented outward thrust. And this Jubilee will be proclaimed so that our Christian brothers and sisters in other lands who speak other languages may know of our love. As a "matter of equality" our abundance shall supply their want.

Unrealistic? Utopian? I suppose so, but some congregations will dare it—why not yours?

Practical Helps

It is good to seek broad sweeping reform; it is also important to find small ways to stimulate one another to love and good works. I therefore conclude this chapter with some simple counsels for the Christian fellowship.

Let us seek to live in compassion and patience with one another. Grace and latitude should mark our relationships. All too often we can injure each other unduly in our zeal for justice and truth and righteousness. The spirit of condemnation can creep into our relationships so subtly. We can begin to look at each other's possessions with a mental calculator. But there is a more excellent way: we simply need to be with one another, loving, supporting, caring. Of course, we live and speak the truth as it has been given to us, but the business of straightening each other out belongs to God, not us.

Let us seek to do "ecclesiastical mercy-killing" wherever we can. Committees and programs that have outlived their usefulness should be given a proper burial. There is no need to complicate the lives of our people with unproductive meetings. Annual reviews that can cut and streamline the church organization will do much to simplify our lives.

Let us seek simple ways to help one another. Many churches have arrangements where people can bring quite good clothing that the children have outgrown so that it can be passed on to families with younger ones. Some churches have food pantries where canned goods and other staples are available to those in need. At harvest time a table can be set out for people to share their surplus garden produce. Some churches have a weekly or monthly "need sheet" where items to sell, buy, or give away can be listed.

Let us seek ways to resurrect the old practice of community "barn-raising." Roofs can be reshingled together. Skills in plumbing, electricity, and carpentry can be swapped. I have seen entire homes built out of the loving labor of the fellowship.

And with the escalating costs of financing today, this may be the only way the younger couples in our fellowship can own a home.

Let us seek to pay our pastors well. Do we fear that they will be taken over by the spirit of greed? No one who has a weakness toward the love of money should be in a pastoral position in the first place (I Tim. 3:3). Let's be known for our gracious generosity to our pastors. It is one way we show our love. It also provides them with the joy of giving to people and causes which they feel are important.

Let us seek to develop many corporate celebrations and feast days. We are enriched by celebrating the goodness of God and our life together. Many such festivals need not be expensive, but some of them should be. We need times when our frugality gives way to the joyous slaying of the "fatted calf." Where I teach we have an annual event called "Symphony of Spring," and the good it does for the human spirit is impossible to calculate. It is the most anticipated event of the year. Music, costumes, color—it is a mini-extravaganza with all the expertise of a professional production, without the plastic superficiality. This event is not cheap. There is a considerable expense in time, energy, and money. We all need such festivals of joy as together we seek the holy simplicity so inherent to the Kingdom of God.

10. CORPORATE SIMPLICITY: THE WORLD

On our crowded planet there are no longer any internal affairs! —*Alexander Solzhenitsyn*

As we face the close of the twentieth century, we need the courage to see the world as it truly is. Many lack this courage. An educated and prosperous professional woman articulated the feelings of vast numbers, "Global consciousness is what I really hate.... It is spoiling my life. I can't stand to have all those pictures of misery, violence and injustice in the world dumped into my living room through the TV."[1] At times we all feel that way. We are overwhelmed by the immensity of the problem and feel helpless to respond.

But we must never succumb to the temptation to self-centered provincialism. We dare not close our eyes to world events by relegating them into neatly packaged eschatological schemes that relieve us of any responsibility. We dare not stop our ears to the sobbing moan of the world's hungry by the insulated assertion that these things must occur before the return of Christ. May God give us eyes to see and ears to hear the world in which we live.

What is our world like? Three billion people have yet to hear the redemption that is in Jesus Christ. Nearly two and one-half billion are culturally outside the present scope of Christian witness. They die without hearing, without knowing. Business as usual will never accomplish the great irrevocable mandate to world evangelization.

What is our world like? We are split between the fat, prosperous affluent and the weak, hungry poor. The gap is widening with alarming speed. Two-thirds of the world, over one hundred nations, suffer chronic food deficiencies while a handful of wealthy nations have attained the highest peaks of material abundance known in the history of humankind.

What is our world like? Nations are irreversibly interdepen dent. The United States now imports nearly 50 percent of its vital resources, and exports vast amounts of food and technology. Any national decision anywhere sends repercussions throughout the globe. Ready or not, like it or not, we are a married world with no divorce possible.

What is our world like? Our planet is plagued by overpopu lation and over-consumption. The net increase in world popula tion now stands at about two hundred thousand a day or seventy-three million per year.[2] No one knows the carrying ca. pacity of our globe but it is likely that we are pushing the lim its. Overpopulation is the problem of the third and fourth World; over-consumption is the problem of the West. The aver age American child this year will consume as much of the world's resources as twenty children born in India.[3] Deliberate and calculated waste is the central aspect of the American economy.[4] We over-eat, over-buy, and over-build, spewing out our toxic wastes upon the earth and into the air.

But this gloomy picture is not the final word. Hope has the final word. We are not locked into a prison of determinism. change is possible. Ruthless inequities can be eradicated. The hungry can be fed. Millions can be reached with the message of life in Christ. He whose power is over all desires to use his peo ple as agents of change. We are to walk cheerfully over the face of the earth, conquering evil with good in the power of the Spirit.

The Principalities and Powers

We who are Christians have a unique contribution to make in solving the vexing global problems, because we have a unique perception of the central issue involved. At the heart of all these complex difficulties is a fundamental spiritual reality. We are not just dealing with facts and figures, people and issues, but with spiritual principalities and powers.

When I speak of these issues as primarily a spiritual reality,

I do *not* mean that all we are to concern ourselves with is saving souls and with personal piety. Far from it! I mean that in back of brutal dictators and unjust policies and corrupt institutions are spiritual principalities and powers. I mean that evil can and does incarnate itself into human structures. I mean that institutions can become nothing more than organized sin.[5]

The reverse is also true. By the power of the Spirit, institutions and structures can be the means of bringing great good and blessing into the lives of human beings. Behind just policies and equitable laws are profound spiritual realities. The spiritual powers or "authorities" (ἐξουσίαις) can be either good as in Romans 12, or evil as in Ephesians 6.

Once we perceive the fundamental spiritual reality which underlies all political, social, and economic issues, we understand why we cannot be indifferent to these matters. We dare not confine our efforts to the private sector of life if we desire to bring the whole Gospel that is in Jesus Christ. Jesus addressed nearly every major social issue of his day in one form or another. If we are to be faithful, we must do the same.

The Apostle Paul calls us to wage the peaceable war of the Lamb against evil principalities and powers. We war against all demonic structures and unjust powers in a manner consistent with the strong weapons of Ephesians 6. We attack sin on every level—personal, social, structural, institutional. Like any war it is waged on all fronts at once. The perimeter of our concern encompasses 360 degrees.

Because we understand that the central issue in all these problems is spiritual and moral, we have a tremendous advantage. We are not distracted by the diversionary skirmishes of the enemy. When we approach an absentee landlord of ghetto apartments, we can speak with authority to the issue of greed, because by the power of Christ we are defeating the demonic powers behind the greed. When we confront political policymakers or corporate executives, we do so with an inward strength born out of prayer and fasting, simplicity and submission.

I do not mean that we are to go around quoting Bible verses at people, or even saying anything religious in the conventional sense. I recall well the meeting five of us had with a senior

White House official over the terribly difficult issues relating to war and peace. We gathered for prayer before the meeting and sought the mind of Christ. In the conference itself no "religious" language was used, but there seemed to be a special sense of the presence of Christ, and truth was spoken, I believe, in the power of God. Did our little meeting change government policy? I do not know, but I do believe that far more was accomplished than if we had come barging in with our own little plans and demands couched in pious platitudes.

To know the underlying spiritual nature of the problem we face gives us hope and courage. From the Gospels to the Epistles to the Apocalypse we are told that Christ has conquered, is conquering, and will continue to conquer all evil powers. Colossians especially lifts high the victory of Christ over all satanic forces: "He disarmed the principalities and powers and made a public example of them, triumphing over them in him" (Col. 2:15).

We are to go in the mighty name of Christ conquering and to conquer, not with the weapons of this evil world—guns and tanks and Trident missile systems—but with the greater weapons of truth and righteousness, peace and faith, prayer and fasting. And we need to understand that these are incredibly strong weapons, "For the weapons of our warfare are not worldly but have divine power to destroy strongholds" (II Cor. 10:4).

Now I have no naive optimism that we are going to solve every problem and eliminate all injustice—that must await the return of Christ. But we have a mandate to invade this present evil age and establish beachheads of light and hope everywhere. And we are promised that the gates of hell will not be able to withstand the onslaughts of the Church.

To know that we are dealing primarily with a spiritual reality also gives us important clues as to our strategy. The work of prayer, for example, should not be shoved off into some pious corner to be used only in connection with devotional concerns. Far from it! When we confront structural evil we do so in a power drawn from divine resources. We go to Congressional hearings on world hunger or town hall hearings on zoning laws praying for the power of the Lord to be over all. When we speak, it is out of the deep reservoir of prayer, which gives both humility and authority to our words.

We now turn our attention to a few of the battle fronts in the Lamb's war that have specific bearing on the Discipline of simplicity: world evangelization, world hunger and overpopulation, over-consumption and pollution, and multinational corporations. We must approach these topics with humility, because they are issues upon which earnest Christians have honest differences. That should not keep us from addressing the issues boldly, but it should keep us from arrogance.

World Evangelization

"Of all the tragic needs of human beings none is greater than their alienation from their Creator and the terrible reality of eternal death for those who refuse to repent and believe." So reads the statement coming out of The Consultation on World Evangelization held in Pattaya, Thailand, in June of 1980. This international gathering of over eight hundred Christian leaders who met as a follow-up to the Lausanne Congress of 1974 continues, "If therefore we do not commit ourselves with urgency to the task of evangelization, we are guilty of an inexcusable lack of human compassion."[6]

They have spoken the truth to us. If we have a Christian world view, we are concerned that people everywhere come to accept Christ as their life. And such phenomenal gains have been made in the past two hundred years that the Church is now firmly established in every continent of the world. But if we are to take seriously the task of world evangelization, we must grapple with a sobering statistic from the U.S. Center on World Mission. They tell us that of the two and one-half billion people yet to be reached, nearly all—five out of six—come from cultural groupings where the church does not have an effective witness. "Culturally distant non-Christians," is the term which they use. They estimate some 16,750 such social groupings. No existing missionary agency or evangelistic work is now reaching these "hidden cultures."

The implication is obvious: we need a great new surge of

cross-cultural evangelism. It happened once in the outbreak of the modern missionary movement with William Carey and others. It happened again at the turn of the twentieth century with the Student Volunteer Movement. It can—it must—happen again.

Today we could be on the brink of a new surge in frontier missions. Inter-Varsity's Mission Convention at Urbana has witnessed a dramatic increase in interest in cross-cultural missions. The number of students who have indicated a willingness to seek God's will concerning their involvement in missions has risen steadily from 1,764 in 1970 to 7,979 in 1979.

The economic resources to match this new wave of missionary interest are available if we will commit ourselves to a simpler lifestyle. Missiologist Ralph Winter tells us that if American Presbyterians would live on the salary of the average Presbyterian minister, two billion dollars would be available, almost three times the present U.S. expenditure for missions.[7] We can do it if we have the will. This is no time for limited vision and pygmy plans. We need resources that will triple our missionary force in order to make a massive assault on this last frontier in Christian missions. Gottfried Osei-Mensah, a leading third world figure in the Lausanne Congress, has called for every one thousand Christians to send one missionary to the unreached peoples. Ralph Winter has proposed that Christians in America voluntarily adopt the same level of support accorded missionaries on furlough and give the extra to frontier missions. He has developed the Order for World Evangelization with exactly that objective in mind. Through this means, a family could actually affiliate themselves with a mission agency and help provide resources to reach the Hidden Peoples of the earth.[8]

As we go, let us clearly understand that global justice places some new requirements upon global evangelism. The Good News must be contextualized into the culture in which it is proclaimed. The Gospel of Jesus Christ has no cultural presuppositions. It welcomes those elements of the culture that are not offensive to the Gospel message and rejects those that are. The enduring task of cross-cultural evangelism is to hammer out the difference.

The Good News must be free of all racism and nationalism. We are global citizens with a global Gospel. Our concern is for the well-being of all peoples of the earth, not the selfish interests of any nation-state.

The Good News must be free of all militarism. It matters little whether the militarism is in defense of the vested interests of the privileged elite or is a modern Zealot movement seeking justice through revolution. We dare not allow the little tin gods of our modern nation-states to draw us into their blasphemous intertribal wars.

The Good News must be given to Christ's favorites, the poor and the helpless. We must go, like the Samaritan, among the bruised and half-dead—to the ghettos of America, to the slums of Brazil, to the refugee camps of Cambodia, to every hovel and hut of the earth.

The Good News must liberate—truly liberate. Those who are in bondage to sin, those who are in bondage to poverty, those who are in bondage to brutal social conditions need to be set free. The liberating Gospel of Christ has not fully come until there is freedom from sin, freedom from economic injustice, freedom from structural evil.

The Good News must come in the power of God. No smooth words, no easy cliches, no enticing gimmicks! All slick image-making advertising campaigns are an offense to the Gospel. Paul said, "The Kingdom of God does not consist in talk but in power" (I Cor. 4:19).

The Good News must be backed by integrity in our lives. We cannot proclaim his love if we close our hearts to the hungry. We cannot proclaim his salvation if we have not been saved from our own greed. Flamboyant, prosperous Christians are an offense to third world peoples by their insensitivity to poverty and human deprivation, whether they come as traveling evangelists or sight-seeing vacationers.

World Hunger

How do you say the word *hunger*? Stop awhile and listen to the inner sob of Carolina Maria de Jesus when her daughter pleaded, "Mama, sell me to Doña Julita, because she has delicious food." Now say the word *hunger*. Step into the hovel of Sebastian and Maria Nascimento and look around. The three-year-old twins lie naked and unmoving on the small cot. They will soon die, the victims of malnutrition. Like me, you want to turn away, but stay and see the quiet little boy. He is a two-year-old whose brain is already vegetating from marasmus, a severe form of malnourishment. Maria tries to speak to you but cannot. The tears of a broken-hearted mother spill down her cheeks.[9] Now say the word *hunger*.

We know little of the world of hunger. We can still choose to escape its sights and sounds. But over half of the world's people are intimately acquainted with its horror—indeed, 460 million people are victims of acute hunger. Ten thousand will die by tomorrow. A million hogs in Indiana have superior housing to a billion humans on this planet. In Calcutta alone 600,000 are perpetually homeless.

The terrible, obscene tragedy in all this is that it is preventable. There is almost unanimous agreement among the experts on world hunger that we can alleviate hunger if we are willing to make the necessary sacrifices. We have the resources. We have the technology. It can be done if we have the will.[10]

However, it cannot be done easily. Major obstacles block the way.

The changes in climate can wreak havoc with whole cultures. The most serious drought in living memory has hit Africa's Sahel. The Sahara Desert has been advancing southward at an estimated four to thirty miles a year. No African country between the tenth and twentieth parallels of latitude has escaped. And Northern Africa is only an extreme example of a pervasive dry-weather pattern that has affected parts of the Middle East, India, South Asia, Northern China, and even Central America.

A gradual cooling trend of the surface temperature of the earth has also been well documented. Since the peak high in 1945, the average surface temperature has fallen about 2.7 degrees Fahrenheit. If the trend continues, scientists are concerned that it could produce agricultural disaster. Scientists are widely divided as to why the change is occurring and whether it is only a temporary cycle or more permanent, but the fact of the change is undisputed.

The capricious decisions of political rulers can mean economic ruin and starvation for millions. Dispossessed men, women, and children flood into refugee camps, the tragic victims of war. Refugees are not new to the human scene, but what is new is the increased numbers. Overconcentrations of population have conspired with the increased savagery of modern warfare upon noncombatants to produce more than fourteen million displaced persons.

Unjust social structures perpetuate a hungry world. In many places the powerful privileged elite manipulate land, money, and political decisions to their advantage. Often foreign aid is given or cut off out of political expediency. International trade and the operations of The International Monetary Fund can contribute to affluence in some countries and poverty in others.

Perhaps one of the most formidable problems in world hunger is overpopulation. If you were born in 1930 and live to the end of this century, the earth's living population will have more than tripled in your lifetime. We grow in numbers the equivalent of the entire U.S. population every three years.

Most of the growth has occurred in the poorer countries. It is estimated that, by the turn of this century, four-fifths of the human race will be living in these countries. This has led the Environmental Fund to propose that food and technical assistance should be suspended from any country that does not control its population growth. The extreme expression of this concern was stated by Johnson Montgomery in the so-called "Lifeboat Theory." In short, this theory maintains that affluent nations, which are obviously in the lifeboat, cannot—indeed, should not—aid population-expanding countries for fear they will overload and sink the boat.

This all sounds quite reasonable until we try to understand the underlying causes of overpopulation. One of the most widely documented concepts in social science is what is called the demographic transition. All of the industrialized countries have experienced this transition, and many of the more advanced third world countries are in the final transition. In brief, it describes the three stages involved in the transition from high birth and death rates to low birth and death rates. The first stage, which is characteristic of all pre-industrial societies, is one of a high birth rate matched by a high death rate. As the society experiences improved health and nutrition it enters the second stage, which maintains a high birth rate but a decreasing death rate resulting in a population explosion. In the third stage, birth rates decrease to match the death rate, resulting in zero population growth. Developing countries are now clearly in the second stage, which is the cause for the population boom.[11]

The reasons for demographic transition are hotly debated among social scientists. But one partial answer is simply that parents depend upon children both to perpetuate the family and to provide for economic and old age security. Once it becomes clear that nine children are not required to ensure that two will live to adulthood, there is a dramatic decrease in the birthrate. But the security to have small families will come only as the benefits of healthy economic growth are spread among the poor. The rise of public education is also cited by many as a crucial factor. The idea that poor countries can attain zero growth by an influx of birth control technology without dealing substantially with the issues of economic and educational well-being is a myth of the privileged elite. Arthur Simon, Executive Director of Bread for the World, says, "Adequate nutrition, health care, literacy, and improved incomes for the poor emerge as the most fundamental remedy to the population problem."[12]

The task is massive, but it is not impossible. Repeatedly, world hunger specialists say that it can be done if we will set ourselves to the task. Wonderful strides have been made by Christian relief organizations such as World Vision, World Concern, Food for the Hungry, and many others. These efforts are good and should receive our generous support. But relief alone will not solve the problem—we need public policies that speak to world hunger.

The 1980 Presidential Commission on World Hunger has urged, as its major recommendation, "that the United States Government make the elimination of hunger *the primary focus of its relationships with the developing countries,* beginning with the decade of the 1980s."[13] Their report has far reaching implications and would mean a major shift in U.S. policy priorities. Among other things, they call for a more liberal trade policy toward developing nations, which would include price stabilizing agreements, a reduction of tariffs, and a Trade Adjustment Act that would make provision for U.S. industries adversely affected. Responding to the commission's concern, Bread For The World has initiated "The Hunger and Global Security Bill," which among other things would provide "U.S. development aid only to countries clearly committed to overcoming hunger and poverty."[14] All these recommendations are sound and the bare minimum we should be doing to solve the hunger problem.

Can more be done? Yes, and it should be. We need to initiate a bold new food policy to answer the cry of world hunger and the need for global security. We need to call upon the United Nations to establish world food banks throughout the earth in which world grain reserves could be gathered and dispersed in emergencies. We need to call upon the United States and other developed nations to make a major shift away from meat and alcohol production and consumption in order to release massive amounts of protein rich grain. We need to call upon the International Fisheries Commissions of the world to search for creative new ways to channel fishing catches into human consumption rather than animal consumption. And we need to call upon the developed nations to share freely and rapidly their intellectual resources, especially in the area of intermediate technology.[15]

In his well-known statement on hunger Jesus said, "I was hungry and you gave me food, I was thirsty and you gave me drink. . . . Truly, I say to you, as you did it to one of the least of these my brethren, you did it to me" (Matt. 25:35, 40). The implication of that passage is devastating: Jesus Christ is starving! Of all people, Christians cannot close their ears to the cry of the hungry, for to feed them is to feed Christ.

Runaway Desire

In *Alice in Wonderland*, there is this significant dialogue between Alice and the Dormouse.

"I wish you wouldn't squeeze so," said the Dormouse, who was sitting next to her. "I can hardly breathe."

"I can't help it," said Alice very meekly: "I'm growing."

"You've no right to grow here," said the Dormouse.

"Don't talk nonsense," said Alice more boldly: "You know you're growing too."

"Yes, but I grow at a reasonable pace," said the Dormouse: "not in that ridiculous fashion."[16]

While the third world must struggle with the problem of unchecked growth, the developed countries must struggle with the problem of unchecked desire.

The idea of unlimited growth and expansion is deeply imbedded in the American psyche. William Ophuls says, "Growth is the secular religion of American society."[17] For us, expansion is always desirable, more is always good, bigger is always better. It pervades all of our thought from our view of the gross national product to the size of our homes.

Economically, the concept of expansion as necessarily desirable has its roots in the philosophic work of Adam Smith and especially his *Wealth of Nations*, published in 1776. For Smith, the purpose of economics was a constantly expanding market, hence anything that would stimulate growth was welcome. In effect, this removed any notion of ethics or morality from economics and replaced it with the concept of an "invisible hand," which would guarantee that the good of the whole was insured if all people would pursue their own self-interest.[18] In Christian theology, of course, the only "invisible hand" is God's, and once we grasp it we discover that it leads away from self-interest to justice and compassion for the poor and oppressed.

The expansionist economy that has grown out of this foundation has four crucial assumptions about the world. First, it is assumed that the pursuit of self-interest will necessarily lead to ultimate social good. Purpose and values should be defined in terms of economic growth. Second, there is hardly any limit to nature's generosity. If the economic balloon is to get bigger and bigger, the good earth must constantly yield the needed amounts of new wealth for expansion to continue. Third, the pursuit of economic self-interest of necessity places a higher priority upon those who are alive than it does on generations yet to be born. Besides, if by its very nature economic expan sion is good, then future generations will benefit from our continued growth. Fourth, since constant economic expansion is by definition good, then any negative side effect is a mere externality. Massive industrial pollution is only an unhappy side effect; it does not call into question the economic theory itself.[19]

The effect of all this has been to define success in terms of an ever increasing gross national product and to react negatively to anything that would retard growth. It has also predisposed us to look favorably upon any growth producing incentive. For example, planned obsolescence has become a way of life in American society, because we have found that it produces economic growth. We are a throw-away culture. Industrial designer Brooks Stevens says, "Our whole economy is based on planned obsolescence."[20]

Vance Packard's *The Waste Makers* makes it indisputably clear that deliberate and calculated waste is a central ingredient in our economy. Many products are "death-dated," that is, they are designed to fall apart or become unrepairable at a specific time. In 1960 the average life expectancy of an American car was about ten years, or roughly half the expected life of a Volkswagen.[21] A major steel company has made available a lead-coated steel which, at an increased cost of eight cents per muffler, would give a product which would last the lifetime of the automobile. Instead, auto makers continue to install mufflers that will need to be replaced in two years.[22] At one point a major light bulb producer made a calculated decision to reduce the life span of one of its bulbs from 1000 to 750 hours.[23]

Where planned obsolescence fails, psychological obsolescence takes over. This has been done with unusual success in the clothing and automobile industry, but is also used with many other products. The sole purpose of psychological obsolescence is to make us want to get a product before the old one has ended its usefulness. Back in 1929, General Motors executive Floyd Allen said, "Advertising is in the business of making people helpfully dissatisfied with what they have in favor of something better. The old factors of wear and tear can no longer be depended upon to a create a demand. They are too slow."[24] In the 1920s, Detroit began pioneering in the concept of the annual model change and has not stopped since. Added to this is the endless variety of products that are virtually the same. We can buy 551 brands of coffee, 177 brands of salad dressing, and 249 brands of soap.[25]

The result of this intentional expendability of items to increase economic growth is the most massive solid-waste disposal problem ever known to humankind. Harry Rothman tells us that, "if the American people and their solid wastes were spread evenly over the United States there would be in each square mile of the nation 56 people surrounded by 54 tons of rubbish which would include: 3 junked cars, 25 discarded tires, 8,500 bottles, 17,000 cans, one ton of plastics, and 8½ tons of paper." The American people are now producing a total of 340 million tons of solid wastes per year.[26]

As you know, that is only the tip of the iceberg. In one short generation we have moved from the steel age to the synthetic age. The world of plastics, chemicals, and pesticides is making a profound and irreversible impact upon our ecosystem. According to *Time* magazine there are now 50,000 chemicals on the market, and almost 35,000 of those used in the United States are classified by the federal Environmental Protection Agency (EPA) as being definitely or potentially hazardous to human health.[27] The Surgeon General of the United States recently reported to the Senate that, "The public health risk associated with toxic chemicals is increasing, and will continue to do so," and buttressed his remarks with a Library of Congress study which concluded that toxic chemicals "are so long lasting and pervasive in the environment that virtually the entire population of the nation, and indeed the world, carries some body burden of one or several of them."[28]

Perhaps one of the most dangerous results of all this is the toxic pollutants that we dump into the atmosphere, and which fall back to the earth as "acid rain." Acid rain is destroying forests, crops, even sea life. According to some studies in the United States, acid rain has reduced cotton yields by 33 percent and tomato harvests by 21 percent."[29] Leon S. Dochinger of the United States Department of Agriculture has said that acid rain "is perhaps the most serious environmental dilemma of this century."[30]

Beyond that is the great danger of destroying the earth's

ozone layer. The National Academy of Sciences warns of a future depletion of the ozone layer of up to 16.5 percent as a result of pollutants dumped into the biosphere.[31]

In spite of all the shortcomings of *The Limits of Growth* report of the Club of Rome, they did shout to us one devastatingly undeniable truth: our "growthmania" must stop or it will destroy us.

We simply must understand that the wonderful resources of the earth are limited. We are now entering the age of scarcity. Jeremy Rifkin, in *The Emerging Order*, goes into extensive detail and documentation to demonstrate that our energy resources are severely limited. He explodes the myth that nuclear energy or solar power or some new technological breakthrough will allow our highly prized expansionism to continue unimpeded. We are reaching the limits of our oil, minable coal, and minerals. Many experts now predict that within seventy-five years or less at current consumption rates we will have "exhausted presently known recoverable reserves of perhaps half the world's now useful metals."[32] Rifkin argues persuasively that even our renewable resources—water, forests, fisheries, crop land, and grazing land—are seriously threatened and being depleted.[33]

The message from all quarters is the same: *our undisciplined consumption must end*. If we continue to gobble up our resources without any regard to stewardship and to spew out our deadly wastes over land, sea, and air, we may well be drawing down the final curtain upon ourselves.

I need to add a reason for curbing our gluttonous consumption that Christians should consider very seriously. Overconsumption is a "cancer eating away at our spiritual vitals."[34] It cuts the heart out of our compassion. It distances us from the great masses of broken bleeding humanity. It converts us into materialists. We become less able to ask the moral questions. For example, just because we have the economic muscle to buy up vast amounts of the world's oil, does that give us the right to do so? When the poor farmer of India is unable to buy a gallon of gasoline to run his simple water pump because the world's demand has priced him out of the market, who is to blame? You see, our sensitivities have been dulled by our over-consumption. Our undisciplined squandering is destroying us spiritually. Walter Harrelson, professor of Old Testament at Vanderbilt University, says, "Overeating and overconsumption, gross inequity in the control of wealth, and a desire to maintain one's own style of life irrespective of world famine clearly constitutes sin in the biblical perspective."[35]

What is urgently needed is a bold new move from a consumer economy to a conserver economy in all of the developed countries, and particularly in the United States. It would mean gargantuan policy shifts in industry and government. It would call for a massive reorientation in the mind-set of the American populace. It would demand a conviction that slowing down (and in certain places cutting back) our growth rate would be advantageous. I am not advocating a "zero-growth economy," but I am suggesting that we need a good dose of temperance.

The task will admittedly be formidable. While it is difficult to control a growth economy, the problems are even greater when attempting to control deliberate economic restraint. I am not an economist, and although I have consulted two highly respected economists in the preparation of this chapter,[36] I do not know all of the problems that a conserver economy would engender. Probably no single individual can understand the full dimensions of this problem.

Therefore, I believe it would be wise at this point in our history for the Christian community to convene an International Congress on Economics and Social Justice. The 1974 Lausanne Congress on World Evangelization has had an important and positive impact. We need a similar gathering of Christian leadership to bring our faith to bear on this issue. We need the insight and guidance such an international gathering could provide. Perhaps they could hammer out some ethical guidelines that would inform our policies and practices. Economists from the various Christian colleges and elsewhere could give significant leadership to such an enterprise.

Christians can make, I think, a unique contribution to this issue, because biblically and theologically we have a vital interest in both stewardship of the earth and economic justice for the poor. And because our allegiance to God is higher than to any nation-state, we have a commitment to global citizenship that can help us transcend the provincial claims of national interest.

Multinational Corporations

At this point, any number of issues could be considered with profit. We could look at the proposals for a New International Economic Order that came out of the General Assembly of the United Nations in May of 1974. We could study the question of international trade as it applies to social justice. We could explore the matter of foreign aid and the policies that could be designed to help the bottom 60 percent of the world. All of these matters are worthy of careful study and thought. I have, however, chosen to deal with the issue of multinational corporations, because they pose both the gravest danger to a more just and equitable world, and potentially the most powerful force for realizing a more just and equitable world.

The era of multinational corporations interjects a new reality into human society. We have always had global visionaries, and businessmen have ventured abroad at least since the Phoenicians began selling glass to their Mediterranean neighbors. What makes the global corporations unique is that for the first time in history, organizations have arisen that have both the ideology and the technology to bring about Wendell Willkie's dream of "One World." Richard Barnet and Ronald Müller, in *Global Reach,* their authoritative study of multinationals, state, "The global corporation is the most powerful human organization yet devised for colonizing the future."[37] And Aurelio Peccei, a director of Fiat and organizer of the Club of Rome, says that the multinational corporation "is the most powerful agent for the internationalization of human society."[38]

Arising out of the post–World War II technological explosion, multinational corporations have had a spectacular growth rate. The Club of Rome reports that, "of the 100 wealthiest entities on the international scene, well over half are corporations."[39] The most successful of the multinational organizations have an annual growth rate that is two to three times that of most industrial countries, including the United States. Barnet and Müller have compared the annual sales of multinational corporations with the gross national product of countries for 1973, and discovered that "GM is bigger than Switzerland, Pakistan, and South Africa; that Royal Dutch Shell is bigger than Iran, Venezuela, and Turkey; and that Goodyear Tire is bigger than Saudi Arabia."[40] Seven oil companies, known as the "Seven Sisters," control over two-thirds of the world's oil and natural gas supply. Professor Howard Perlmutter, of the Wharton School, estimates that by 1986, two to three hundred global corporations will control eighty percent of of all productive assets of the non-Communist world.[41]

The global corporations can exert tremendous political and economic clout throughout the world. The economic sanctions, for example, of the countries of the world against the Chilean junta of Augusto Pinochet has had little effect because the multinational banks have loaned the Chilean government some one billion dollars. Hence, the junta has been able to laugh at the international human rights campaign that had been mounted against its brutal violations of civil liberties.[42] Because the multinational corporations often function as monopolies or oligarchies, they can control the supply of resources that is crucial to the survival of nations even as large as the United States.

These corporations are highly mobile, and often build duplicate production facilities in different countries in order to move quickly to avoid stringent antipollution laws, high wage demands, or other economically disadvantageous situations. While such mobility works to the economic benefit of the corporation, it can be devastating to a local economy. In the early 1970s, General Instruments cut its New England labor force by three thousand and increased its force in Taiwan by almost five thousand. Singer Sewing Machine reduced its main American plant in New Jersey from ten thousand employees to two thousand.[43] Their mobility has robbed labor of its traditional bargaining powers, which explains why organized labor has been consistently critical of multinationals.

The most distinctive feature of what Barnet and Müller call "the World Managers" is not their size, but their ability to transcend any given nation-state. The concerns for growth and profits take precedence over the interests of any nation, including the country of their origin. Antitrust regulations and other laws designed to regulate what occurs within a nation prove worthless in controlling the activities of multinationals. Hence, national governments find it increasingly difficult to keep these global corporations from determining what goes on in the world.

Multinationals are not accountable to any nation, nor do they feel a responsibility for the welfare of any nation. They can buy up huge, tillable land masses to grow sugar cane for export without any regard for what that might mean in terms of food production for the people. They can launch large advertising campaigns to convince the poorest of the world that formula milk is to be preferred to breast milk without regard for sanitary conditions among the poor, or for the couple's ability to buy an adequate supply of milk for their child.[44]

The global corporations respond that they are the architects of world peace and prosperity. By interlinking the economies of the earth, they feel they are producing a world that is so interdependent that war is an increasing impossibility. They claim to be producing job markets and increased wealth throughout the world.

Will the era of global corporations institute a new form of imperial domination, or will it usher in a new golden age? No one knows for certain, but two things are clear. First, multinational corporations have the resources and the organization to bring immeasurable benefits to the human family. Second, this will never occur unless some form of strict accountability is placed upon multinationals.

There is need for an international monitoring of the activities of global corporations, perhaps through the United Nations. They must be forced by law to reveal all the relevant facts of their operations which are now concealed. An international Code of Conduct needs to be developed to regulate the operations of multinationals. For example, a policy should be adopted which would insist that there be an economic inflow into a country to match what is extracted from it. Also, the cost of raw materials should have an equitable tie to the purchase price of the finished product.

Strict *international* environmental standards must be set to govern the activities of multinational corporations. Environmental impact studies must be mandatory, with strict and universal antipollution regulations.

These and many more areas of accountability are needed if the global corporations are to benefit society with a generosity equal to their profit margin.[45]

How Can I Help?

It is easy to feel that these issues are far beyond our small abilities, but there is much that we can do.* First, we can open ourselves to the possibility that God may well want to use us in a large way. History is full of ordinary people who, like Amos, were called to positions of influence far beyond their intentions. Second, we can get the facts. We become global citizens by caring enough to be informed about what happens to our neighbors in Chile and Mozambique. Third, we can become advocates of the powerless and exploited. Our comfortable dinner parties and Sunday School classes need to hear the whimpering cry of the poor. We are strong on love, but soft on justice.

Fourth, we can support relief agencies in their good work. They need our help. Fifth, we can go beyond relief and become involved politically. Life is political; and if we refuse to influence public policy, someone else will. Sixth, we can use our literary skills in the cause of the poor. Letters to the editor, newsletters, magazine articles, good books are all needed. Our hymns and gospel songs need social content. We must write forcefully, honestly, tenderly. Seventh, the ministry of prayer must be taken into the social arena. It is hard work, but necessary to defeat the demonic principalities and powers infesting so many social institutions.

The brief words of this chapter have only touched the edge of the many ways simplicity speaks to the world in which we live. May Jesus Christ, our ever present Teacher, continue to instruct us in how to apply his life-giving Gospel to every institution and structure in human society.

---

* I am indebted to T. Wayne Rieman of Manchester College, Indiana, for several of these practical suggestions.

THE SIMPLICITY
OF SIMPLICITY

At the beginning of this book I underscored the complexity of our task. There simply are no easy answers to the tough questions of how we are to relate with integrity to the modern world. The difficulty of our task is evident enough on the personal level, but the moment we begin to deal with the broader issues of church and state and international relations we are staggered by the immense complexity of simplicity.

It is essential for us to be confronted by this reality if we are to escape superficiality. But there is a danger in understanding the intricacies of these issues. Once we begin to see the complexity of it all, we can become overwhelmed. We despair of ever being able to fit the pieces of the puzzle together. We find ourselves struggling on the personal level with our dishonest speech and obsessive status-seeking and compulsive extravagance—not to mention the complex matters of economics and global hunger and international trade. It is easy to become immobilized by the enormity of our task. Discouragement and then despair can set in all too quickly. Without anyone noticing, we quietly resign ourselves to the status quo: "I can't change the world and I'm not even sure I can (or want) to change my own lifestyle, so I'd better leave things as they are. Nothing ventured, nothing lost!"

But it is exactly at that point that we are tragically mistaken. We have a great deal to lose! Simplicity is part and parcel of our call to be a disciple of Jesus Christ. It is not an "extra" that we can tack onto our Christian experience as we add a tape deck to a new car. It is an essential part of the Classical Disciplines of the Christian life. Simplicity is essential in the way that wheels or brakes or an engine are essential to an automobile; without them there is no functional automobile. Simplicity is essential in the way that prayer and worship or any of the Spiritual Disciplines are essential; without them there is no functional disciple of Christ.

The Spiritual Disciplines (of which simplicity is a vital part) are the conduit through which our obedience flows; they are visible ways by which we express our discipleship. And more importantly, they set us before God in such a way that we can be transformed and conformed to the way of Christ. William Penn said, "To be like Christ, then, is to be a Christian,"[1] which is precisely why simplicity is such an important part of Christian devotion. Nothing is more clear than that Jesus Christ walked in a well-nigh amazing simplicity of life. He was centered in God and had a transparency toward God that ordered everything. Simplicity is part of what it means to be a follower of Christ.

To be sure, the cost of simplicity is great, but the cost of duplicity is greater. Duplicity costs the joyful communion with the divine Center, faith that sees everything in the light of God's governance for good, abiding peace, and the ability to walk cheerfully over the face of the earth in the power of the Lord. In short, it costs the abundant life Jesus said he came to bring. Simplicity may be difficult, but the alternative is immensely more difficult.

The joyful paradox in all this is that while simplicity is complex it is also simple. In the final analysis we are not the ones who have to untangle all the intricacies of our complex world. There are not many things we have to keep in mind—in fact, only one: to be attentive to the voice of the true Shepherd. There are not many decisions we have to make—in fact, only one: to seek first his Kingdom and his righteousness. There are not many tasks we have to do—in fact, only one: to obey him in all things. As Søren Kierkegaard understood so clearly, we are honed down to only one thing, and that is the simplicity of simplicity.

This is why the inward reality of holy obedience to the divine Center is so central to everything about simplicity.

Without that we will become frustrated and stymied by the complexity of it all. With it life is ordered and filled with peace. The only thing we have to do is be, at every moment, attentive to the heavenly Monitor. And as we are, there come welling up whispers of divine guidance and love that make life radiant.

Jesus invited people to share his yoke, adding that his yoke was easy and his burden was light. A horse or ox is trained to work peaceably and well by being yoked or harnessed to one already trained. At first the untrained animal may chafe under the yoke, and try to bolt away. So long as he does, the yoke will be a heavy burden indeed. But as he learns to walk step by step with the trained animal, he learns to walk with ease.

We too are yoked to One who is trained. Our only task is to keep in step with him. He chooses the direction and leads the way. As we walk step by step with him, we soon discover that we have lost the crushing burden of needing to take care of ourselves and get our own way, and we discover that the burden is indeed light. We come into the joyful, simple life of hearing and obeying.

NOTES

Chapter 1. The Complexity of Simplicity

[1] W. Stanley Mooneyham, *What Do You Say to a Hungry World?* (Waco: Word Publishing Co., 1975), p. 32.

[2] Thomas Kelly, *A Testament of Devotion* (New York: Harper & Row Publishers, 1941), p. 124.

[3] Pope John XXIII, *Journal of a Soul*, trans. Dorothy White (New York: McGraw-Hill Book Co., 1965), pp. 278–279.

[4] Dietrich Bonhoeffer, *Ethics*, ed. Eberhard Bethge (New York: The Macmillan Co., 1955), p. 68.

[5] *Celebration of Discipline* (New York: Harper & Row, 1978). The Spiritual Disciplines discussed in that book are meditation, prayer, fasting, study, simplicity, solitude, submission, service, confession, worship, guidance, and celebration. They are described as "classical" not because they are ancient but because they are central to experiential Christianity.

When *Celebration of Discipline* was being prepared for publication many different subtitles had been proposed; hence I was unaware of the final decision. When I received the examination copy of the dustjacket I groaned. The subtitle was, "Paths to Spiritual Growth." That subtitle missed a crucial point. The Disciplines are not independent "paths" as if you can exercise one without the other. Like the fruit of the Spirit they constitute a unity: not "fruits" but "fruit," not "paths" but "path." I wrote an impassioned plea requesting that the plural be changed to a singular, which graciously the house of Harper & Row consented to do.

[6] François Fénelon, *Christian Perfection* (New York: Harper & Brothers, 1947), p. 194.

[7] Ibid.

Chapter 2. The Biblical Roots: The Old Covenant

[1]See the article "The OT Term מִשְׁפָּט in *Theological Dictionary of the New Testament* (Grand Rapids: William B. Eerdmans Publishing Co., 1975). Expanded information on the use of *mishpat* in the Old Testament can be found in this excellent article.

[2]There are many excellent word studies of *shalom* in standard volumes. A very helpful booklet is Howard Macy, *The Shalom of Goa* (Richmond; Friends United Press, 1973). Two books which deal with *Shalom* in the context of Christian simplicity are John V. Taylor, *Enough Is Enough* (cited below) and Richard K. Taylor, *Economics and the Gospel* (Philadelphia: United Church Press, 1973).

[3]John V. Taylor, *Enough Is Enough* (Minneapolis: Augsburg Publishing House, 1977), p. 42.

Chapter 3. The Biblical Roots: The New Covenant

[1]I am indebted to Dallas Willard of the University of Southern California for the many insights into Matthew 6 that he has given me through both his life and his teaching.

[2]The discussions as to the meaning of ἁπλοῦς are quite involved. An excellent summary of the issue can be found in an unpublished doctoral dissertation by Carol Schaefer, *A Study in the Exegesis of Matt. 6:22 Through an Analysis of Haplous* (Providence: Brown University, 1963). Also of interest is an excellent exegesis of Matt. 6:22-24 by Mark Silliman, *The Dark Amen Versus the Light AMEN* (Wichita: Friends University, 1980). My use of the passage follows the lead of John Wesley, who felt *haplous* referred to a single aim in life, namely God. He used the text to defend the glories of being poor and simple with God, versus rich and godless.

Dallas Willard, in a lecture on the Sermon on the Mount, Spring 1974, Woodlake Avenue Friends Church, Canoga Park, California.

[4]Martin Hengel, *Property and Riches in the Early Church* (Philadelphia: Fortress Press, 1973), p. 27.

Chapter 4. Simplicity Among the Saints

[1]Quoted in D. Elton Trueblood, *The Best of Elton Trueblood: An Anthology,* ed. James R. Newby (Nashville: The Benson Co., 1979), p. 70.

[2]John Woolman, *The Journal of John Woolman* (Secaucus: The Citadel Press, 1972), p. 41.

[3]Quoted in Martin Hengel, *Property and Riches in the Early Church* (Philadelphia: Fortress Press, 1973), p. 45.

[4]Tertullian, "The Apology of Tertullian" in Alexander Roberts and James Donaldson, eds. *The Ante-Nicene Fathers,* 8 vols. (Buffalo: The Christian Literature Publishing Co., 1887), 3:46.

[5] "The Teaching of the Twelve Apostles" in Roberts and Donaldson, *The Ante-Nicene Fathers*, 7:378.

[6] Eusebius, *The Ecclesiastical History*, trans. Christian Frederick Cruse, reprint ed. (Grand Rapids: Baker Book House, 1958), Book IV, Chapter 23, p. 160.

[7] "The First Epistle of Clement to the Corinthians" in Roberts and Donaldson, *The Ante-Nicene Fathers*, 1:15.

[8] "Epistle of Clement to James" in Roberts and Donaldson, *The Ante-Nicene Fathers*, 8:220.

[9] Quoted in *Quotations from Chairman Jesus*, ed. David Kirk (Springfield: Templegate Publishers, 1969), p. 175.

[10] "The First Apology of Justin Martyr" in Roberts and Donaldson, *The Ante-Nicene Fathers*, 1:186.

[11] Ibid., pp. 42–43.

[12] Quoted by Henri Nouwen in "The Desert Counsel to Flee the World," *Sojourners*, 9 (June 1980):15.

[13] Helen Waddell, trans., *The Desert Fathers* (Ann Arbor: The University of Michigan Press, 1957), p. 85.

[14] Quoted by Henri Nouwen, "Silence, The Portable Cell," *Sojourners* 9 (July 1980):22.

[15] Waddell, *The Desert Fathers*, p. 123.

[16] Ibid., p. 112.

[17] Paul Sabatier, *Life of St. Francis of Assisi* (New York: Charles Scribner's Sons, 1894), p. 83.

[18] Ibid., p. 114.

[19] Ibid., p. 307.

[20] Raphael Brown, trans., *The Little Flowers of St. Francis* (Garden City; Doubleday & Company, 1958), p. 68.

[21] Ibid., pp. 81–82.

[22] Ibid., pp. 58–60.

[23] Theodore G. Tappert, ed., *Selected Writings of Martin Luther: 1520–1523* (Philadelphia: Fortress Press, 1967), p. 20.

[24] Ibid., p. 37.

[25] Ibid., p. 43.

[26] Ibid., p. 47.

[27] John Calvin, *Commentaries on the Epistle of Paul the Apostle to the Romans* (Grand Rapids: Wm. B. Eerdmans Publishing Co., 1947), p. 481.

[28] George Fox, *The Journal of George Fox* (London: Cambridge University Press, 1952), p. 11.

[29] Quoted in Lewis Benson, *A Revolutionary Gospel* (Philadelphia: The Tract Association of Friends, 1974), p. 9.

[30] William Penn, *No Cross, No Crown* (London: Richard Barrett, printer, 1857), p. 251.

[31] George Fox, *Works of George Fox*, reprint ed. (Philadelphia: Marcus T. C. Gould, 1831), 4:194.

[32] Hugh Barbour and Arthur Roberts, eds., *Early Quaker Writings* (Grand Rapids: William B. Eerdmans Publishing Co., 1973), p. 115.

[33] Taken from the bulletin of the First Centenary United Methodist Church, Chattanooga, Tennessee, June 29, 1980, p. 1.

[34] John Wesley, *The Journal of John Wesley*, ed. Percy Livingstone Parker (Chicago: Moody Press, 1951), p. 409.

[35] Francis Asbury, *The Journal of Francis Asbury* (London: Epworth Press, 1958), 1:4.

[36] Howard Taylor, *Hudson Taylor's Spiritual Secret* (Chicago: Moody Press, 1932), p. 26.

[37] Kenneth Scott Latourette, *A History of Christianity* (New York: Harper & Brothers, 1953), p. 1186.

[38] J. H. Worcester, *The Life of David Livingstone* (Chicago: Moody Press, n.d.), p. 75.

[39] Ibid., p. 100.

[40] For more information see Dallas Lee, *The Cotton Patch Evidence* (New York: Harper & Row, 1971).

[41] Girolamo Savonarola, *De Simplicitate Christianae Vitae* (Rome: Angelo Belardetti Editore Roma, n.d.,), p. 188. Unfortunately, this book has never been translated into English. I am indebted to Father Lawrence F. Frankovich (O.F.M.) for help in translating crucial sections of this book.

[42] Ibid., pp. 64–65.

[43] Søren Kierkegaard, *Purity of Heart Is to Will One Thing* (New York: Harper & Brothers, 1938), p. 27.

[44] Ibid., p. 29.

[45] Woolman, *The Journal of John Woolman*, p. 41.

[46] Ibid., p. 168.

[47] Ibid., p. 231.

[48] Quoted in Goldian VanderBroeck, ed., *Less Is More* (New York: Harper & Row, 1978), p. 223.

Chapter 5. Inward Simplicity: The Divine Center

[1] J. R. R. Tolkien, *The Silmarillion* (New York: George Allen & Unwin, 1977), p. 8.

[2] Kelly, *A Testament of Devotion*, p. 115.

[3] Ibid.

[4] Ibid., pp. 115–116.

[5] Quoted in Francis Florand, *Stages of Simplicity* (St. Louis: B. Herder Book Co., 1967), p. 147.

[6] I am indebted to Thomas Kelly for the concept of many inward selves. See *A Testament of Devotion*, pp. 114–115.

[7] Frank Laubach, *Learning the Vocabulary of God* (Nashville: The Upper Room, 1956), p. 5.

[8] Ibid., p. 23.

[9] Brother Lawrence (Nicholas Herman of Lorraine), *The Practice of the Presence of God* (Philadelphia: The Judson Press, n.d.), p. 26.

[10] Meister Eckhart, *Meister Eckhart*, trans. C. de B. Evans (London: John M. Watkins, 1956) 1:59.

[11] Quoted in Frank C. Laubach, *Christ Liveth in Me* and *Games with Minutes*, in 1 vol. (Westwood: Fleming H. Revell Co., 1961), p. 61.

[12] Kelly, *A Testament of Devotion*, p. 124.

[13] Blaise Pascal, *Pensees*, trans. W. F. Trotter, The Modern Library (New York: Random House, 1941), p. 74.

[14] Wayne E. Oates, *Nurturing Silence in a Noisy Heart* (Garden City: Doubleday & Co., 1979), p. 3.

[15] Frank C. Laubach, *Open Windows, Swinging Doors* (Glendale: Gospel Light Publications, 1955), pp. 34–35.

[16] Fénelon, *Christian Perfection*, p. 204.

Chapter 6. Inward Simplicity: Holy Obedience

[1] T. S. Eliot, *The Four Quartets* (New York: Harcourt, Brace & World, Inc., 1943), p. 39.

[2] Quoted in Kelly, *A Testament of Devotion*, p. 52.

[3] Fénelon, *Christian Perfection*, p. 196.

[4] Ibid.

[5] Ibid., p. 194.

[6] Ibid.

[7] Brother Lawrence, *The Practice of the Presence of God*, p. 39.

[8] Fénelon, *Christian Perfection*, p. 196.

[9] Ibid., pp. 198–199.

[10] Ibid., p. 201.

[11] Ibid., p. 203.

[12] Ibid., p. 204.

[13] Ibid., p. 197.

[14] Julian of Norwich, *Showings* (New York: Paulist Press, 1978), p. 205.

[15] Blaise Pascal, *Love Aflame: Selections from the Writings of Blaise Pascal* (Wilmore: Asbury Theological Seminary, 1974), p. 3.

[16] Kelly, *A Testament of Devotion*, p. 69.

[17] Søren Kierkegaard, *Christian Discourses,* trans. Walter Lowie (Oxford: Oxford University Press, 1940), p. 322.

[18] In a letter written to U.S. Senator Mark Hatfield as a response to his congratulatory letter to her upon her receipt of the Nobel Peace Prize. Published in *Major Addresses Delivered at the Conference on Faith and Learning* (North Newton: Bethel College, 1980), pp. 85–86.

Chapter 7. Outward Simplicity: Beginning Steps

[1] One especially helpful book is by George Fooshee, *You Can Be Financially Free* (Old Tappan: Fleming H. Revell Co., 1976).

[2] Catherine de Hueck Doherty, *Poustinia: Christian Spirituality of the East for Western Man* (Notre Dame: Ave Maria Press, 1974), p. 216.

[3] Quoted in VanderBroeck, *Less Is More,* p. 26.

[4] Richard E. Byrd, *Alone* (New York: G. P. Putnam's Sons, Inc., 1938), p. 19.

[5] John Wesley, "Nov. 1767," *The Journal of the Reverend John Wesley* (London: The Epworth Press, 1938).

[6] Quoted in VanderBroeck, *Less Is More,* p. 21.

Chapter 8. Outward Simplicity: Longer Strides

[1] Adam Daniel Finnerty, *No More Plastic Jesus* (New York: E. P. Dutton Inc., 1978), p. 17.

[2] John Stott, *Lausanne Occasional Papers, No. 3: The Lausanne Covenant—An Exposition and Commentary* (Wheaton: Lausanne Committee for World Evangelism, 1975), p. 21.

[3] Floyd and Norma Souders, *Friends University: 1898–1973* (North Newton: Mennonite Press, 1974), p. 11.

[4] Quoted in John Mitchell, *Enough Is as Good as a Feast* (An offset from *Third Way Magazine,* London, England, 1979), p. 1.

[5] Elizabeth O'Connor, *Letters to Scattered Pilgrims* (San Francisco: Harper & Row, 1979), p. 5.

[6] Ibid., pp. 6–7.

[7] Mooneyham, *What Do You Say to a Hungry World?* p. 76.

[8] Woolman, *The Journal of John Woolman,* p. 18.

[9] Ibid.

[10] Thomas Merton, *The Sign of Jonas* (New York: Harcourt, Brace and Co., 1953), p. 261.

[11] Jacques Ellul, *Violence: Reflections from a Christian Perspective* (New York: The Seabury Press, 1969), p. 151.

[12] Ibid., p. 155.

[13] Kierkegaard, *Christian Discourses*, p. 344.

[14] Quoted in VanderBroeck, *Less Is More*, p. 70.

[15] Ibid., p. 127.

Chapter 9. Corporate Simplicity: The Church

[1] Quoted in *Post-American* 1 (Summer 1972): 1.

[2] Douglas V. Steere, ed., *Selections from the Writings of Bernard of Clairvaux* (Nashville: The Upper Room, 1961), p. 6.

[3] Quoted by Leland Ryken, in "The Puritan Work Ethic: The Dignity of Life's Labors," in *Christianity Today*, Oct. 19, 1979, p. 17.

[4] Lee, *The Cotton Patch Evidence*, pp. 86–87.

[5] This illustration was suggested to me by Kara Cole in *The Church— Every Person a Minister* (Dublin: Prinit Press, 1980), pp. 11–13.

Chapter 10. Corporate Simplicity: The World

[1] James Scherer, *Global Living Here and Now* (New York: Friendship Press, 1974), p. 6.

[2] Jeremy Rifkin, with Ted Howard, *The Emerging Order* (New York: G. P. Putnam's Sons, 1979), p. 58.

[3] Ibid., p. 60.

[4] Finnerty, *No More Plastic Jesus*, p. 34.

[5] This issue is dealt with in detail in Oscar Cullmann, *The State in the New Testament*, and in Hendrikus Berkhof, *Christ and the Powers*. See also "The Powers of Evil in the New Testament" in the *Evangelical Quarterly* 52, no. 2 (April–June 1980). I have dealt at length with this topic in Chapter 5 of *Quaker Concern in Race Relations: Then and Now*, D.Th.P. diss., Fuller Theological Seminary, 1970).

[6] "The Thailand Statement," *World Evangelization*, Information Bulletin No. 20, a publication of the Lausanne Committee for World Evangelization, September 1980, p. 6.

[7] Ralph D. Winter, *Penetrating the Last Frontiers* (Pasadena: William Carey Library, 1978), pp. 50–52.

[8] Ibid., pp. 49–52. See also Ralph D. Winter, *Six Essential Components of World Evangelization: Goals for 1984* (Pasadena: William Carey Library, 1979), pp. 15–18.

[9] Mooneyham, *What Do You Say to a Hungry World?* pp. 47–48.

[10] The statistics given in the section on world hunger are readily available in most books on the subject. Examples are *The Challenge of World Poverty* by Gunnar Myrdal, *Bread for the World* by Arthur Simon, *The Emerging Order* by Jeremy Rifkin, and *What Do You Say To A Hungry World?* by W. Stanley Mooneyham (publication information for these books is cited elsewhere in these notes).

[11] Bee-Lan Chan Wang, "The Population and Food Dilemma: Christian Perspectives," in *A Reader in Sociology: Christian Perspectives,* ed. Charles De Santo, Calvin Redekop and William Smith-Hinds (Scottdale: Herald Press, 1980), pp. 446–448.

[12] Arthur Simon, *Bread for the World* (Grand Rapids: Wm. B. Eerdmans Publishing Co., 1975), p. 31.

[13] The Presidential Commission on World Hunger, *Overcoming World Hunger: The Challenge Ahead,* 734 Jackson Place, NW, Washington, D.C. 20006, Ambassador Sol M. Linowitz, Chairman, March 1980, p. ix.

[14] *Hunger and Global Security,* flier printed by Bread for the World, 32 Union Square East, New York, New York 10003.

[15] For further information on the subject of world hunger see Gunnar Myrdal, *The Challenge of World Poverty* (New York: Random House, 1971), Jayne Millar, *Focusing on Global Poverty and Development* (Overseas Development Council, 1974), and Freudenberger and Minus, *Christian Responsibility in a Hungry World* (Nashville: Abingdon Press, 1976).

[16] Lewis Carroll, *Alice in Wonderland,* ed. Donald J. Gray (New York: W. W. Norton & Co. Inc., 1971), pp. 88–89.

[17] William Ophuls, *Ecology and the Politics of Scarcity* (San Francisco: W. H. Freeman & Co., 1977), p. 185.

[18] Adam Smith, *The Wealth of Nations,* The Modern Library (New York: Random House, 1937), p. 423.

[19] These four assumptions are taken from the analysis of Smith's economic thought by Jeremy Rifkin, *The Emerging Order,* pp.-35–36.

[20] Quoted in Vance Packard, *The Waste Makers* (New York: McKay, 1960), p. 54.

[21] Ibid., p. 24.

[22] Ibid., p. 99.

[23] Harvey Salgo, "The Obsolescence of Growth: Capitalism and the Environmental Crisis," in *The Review of Radical Political Economics* 5 (Fall 1973): 32.

[24] Ibid., p. 31.

[25] Packard, *The Waste Makers,* p. 228.

[26] Harry Rothman, *Murderous Providence: A Study of Pollution in Industrial Societies* (New York: Bobbs-Merrill Co., 1972), p. 64.

[27] Ed Magnuson, "The Poisoning of America," in *Time* 116 (September 22, 1980): 58.

[28] Ibid.

[29] "Fine Particles in the Atmosphere," *NRDC Newsletter* 7, nos. 2, 3 (March 1978–June 1978), Natural Resources Defense Council, p. 8.

[30] Ward Sinclair, "Studies Warn About Menace of 'Acid Rain,' " *Washington Post*, June 2, 1978, p. A18.

[31] Worldwatch Institute, "The Global Environment and Basic Human Needs," report to the U.S. Council on Environmental Quality, 1978, p. 42.

[32] Preston Cloud, "Mineral Resources in Fact and Fancy," in *Toward a Steady-State Economy*, ed. Herman E. Daly (San Francisco: W. H. Freeman & Co., 1973), p. 74.

[33] Rifkin, *The Emerging Order*, pp. 47–65.

[34] T. Wayne Rieman, "A Christian Response in a Global Community," (paper, Manchester College, September 14, 1976).

[35] Walter Harrelson, "Famine in the Perspective of Biblical Judgments and Promises," in *Lifeboat Ethics: The Moral Dilemmas of World Hunger*, ed. George Lucas and Thomas Ogletree (New York: Harper & Row Publishers, 1976), p. 93.

[36] Kenneth Boulding of the University of Colorado and Donald Hay of Oxford University, England. Though space prohibited my discussion of it, I am particularly indebted to Professor Boulding's *The Economy of Love and Fear*, which is an introductory study in Grants Economics. See also his *Redistribution to the Rich and the Poor* and *Transfers in an Urbanized Economy*. These two gentlemen are in no way responsible for the conclusions I have drawn.

[37] Richard Barnet and Ronald Müller, *Global Reach: The Power of the Multinational Corporations* (New York: Simon & Schuster, 1974), p. 363.

[38] Ibid., p. 13.

[39] Ervin Lastlo et al., *Goals for Mankind* (New York: New American Library, 1978), p. 165.

[40] Barnet & Müller, *Global Reach*, p. 15.

[41] Mark Green and Robert Massie, eds., *The Big Business Reader* (New York: The Pilgrim Press, 1980), p. 381.

[42] Ibid., pp. 399–412.

[43] Barnet and Müller, *Global Reach*, p. 22.

[44] Green and Massie, *The Big Business Reader*, pp. 418–429.

[45] Other specific proposals for bringing accountability to multinational corporations can be found in *Reshaping the International Order: Report to the Club of Rome* (Chapter 15), and Barnet and Müller, *Global Reach* (Chapter 13).

Epilogue: The Simplicity of Simplicity

[1] William Penn, *A Collection of the Works of William Penn*, vol. 1 (London: 1726), p. 840.

Scripture Index

Subject Index

Abraham, 17, 18; generosity of, 24; obedience of, 94; and tithing, 22–23
Accommodation without compromise, 113–15
Activities, recording and ranking of, 91–92
Affluence, 17–18. *See also* Wealth
Agatho, Abbot, 58
Africa, 170; slave trade in, 68–69
Alice in Wonderland, 173–74
Allen, Floyd, 175
American Indians, 67, 140
Amos, 148
Anthony, Saint, 56, 58
Anxiety, 12, 34
Asbury, Francis, 66–67
Augustine of Hippo, 52
Automobiles, 175

Barclay, Robert, 52
Barnabas, 44
Barnet, Richard, 179–80
Baxter, Richard, 52, 148, 149
Beatitudes of Luke, 38–39
Berkeley Christian Coalition, 69
Bernard of Clairvaux, 148
Blessings, and obedience, 20
Bonhoeffer, Dietrich, 10, 42
Booth, William, 68
Brainerd, David, 67
Bread for the World, 172, 173
Budgets: of churches, 160; of families, 118–21
Byrd, Richard E., 123

Calvin, John, 63–64
Carey, William, 67, 168
Catholic Worker Movement, 69
Celibacy, 61, 136–37
Center of life, 78–80, 98, 184
Chesterton, G. K., 110
Children, 137, 141–42; financial education of, 144–45; parental economic dependence on, 172
Christian approach to world problems, 164–67
Christians, early: charity and sharing by, 53–55; fellowship of, 43–46; persecution of, 55

Chrysostom, John, 54
Church, early, 43, 44; care of Hellenistic widows by, 47; charity by, 54–55. *See also* Christians, early
Churches: architecture and construction of, 152–54; "care groups" of, 155; methods to promote economic equality, 159–60; programs to promote Christian fellowship, 161
Church of the Redeemer, 139–40
Church of the Saviour, 132
Church, the: literature on simplicity, 69–73; teaching ministry of, 147–50
Clothes, purchase of, 125–26
Club of Rome, 179
Commitment, and decision-making, 92–93
Communal living, 139–40
"Communion of saints," 52, 73
Communion with God, 82–87
Compassion, 58; and justice, 27–28; in the Old Testament, 27–30
Compromise, 113–15
Constantine, Emperor, 56
Consultation on World Evangelization, 167
Consumerism, 114–15, 121–26
Contentment, 87–89
Corinthians, 47–48
Corporations, multinational, 179–82
Covetousness, 18, 41; vs. contentment, 87–88
Creation, 16–17, 18
Cross-cultural missions, 168–69
Culture: and global evangelism, 168–69; and norms of simplicity, 112–13, 114

Davis, James, 130
Decision-making, 81–82; based on communion with God, 82–83, 156–57; role of commitment in, 92–93
Demographic transition, and overpopulation, 171–72
Dependence on God, 16–17
Descartes, R., 71
Desert Fathers, 55–58
Detachment, 57
Developing countries, U.S. relations with 172–73
Didache, the, 53

A Leader's Guide is available for *Freedom of Simplicity*

Harper's Adult Study Leader's Guides have been prepared for a wide range of books suitable for adult discussion groups.

The Leader's Guide for *Freedom of Simplicity* provides an adult discussion group with step-by-step instructions, discussion questions, journaling exercises, and group activities for a six-session program.

The Leader's Guide makes it easy to conduct lively, stimulating discussion programs that participants will respond to with enthusiasm.

Freedom of Simplicity, Leader's Guide
64 pages, paperback
Richard J. Foster
0-06-062857-X
$5.00

The *Freedom of Simplicity* Leader's Guide is available from your local bookstore or from:

Customer Service Department
HarperSanFrancisco
1160 Battery Street
San Francisco, CA 94111-1213
800-328-5125